CATEGORIES AND CLASSIFICATIONS

MAUSSIAN REFLECTIONS ON THE SOCIAL

N.J. Allen

Berghahn Books
New York • Oxford

First published in 2000 by **Berghahn Books**

www.berghahnbooks.com

©2000 N.J. Allen

Library of Congress Cataloging-in-Publication Data

Allen, N. J.
    Categories and classifications : Maussian reflections on the social /
    N.J. Allen.
       p. cm. – (Methodology and history in anthropology : v. 8)
    Includes bibliographical references and index.
    ISBN 1-57181-808-1 – ISBN 1-57181-824-3 (alk. paper)
    1. Mauss, Marcel, 1872–1950. 2. Ethnology–Philosophy.
    3. Classifications. I. Title. II. Series.

GN21.M33 A45 2000
305.8'001–dc21   00-052995

British Library Cataloguing in Publication Data

A catalogue record for this book is available from the British Library.

Printed in the United States on acid-free paper.

ISBN 1-57181-808-1 hardback
       1-57181-824-3 paperback

To Sheila

CONTENTS

LIST OF FIGURES

ACKNOWLEDGEMENTS

I should like to thank David Parkin for originally suggesting this book, and Bill Pickering for nurturing an early interest in Mauss and the Durkheimian school. Chapter 1 originally appeared in Carrithers, Collins and Lukes (eds) 1985, and is reprinted here by permission of the publishers, Cambridge University Press. Many friends and colleagues have given help or encouragement, or offered useful suggestions, and the following list cannot hope to be complete: Michael Carrithers, Steve Collins, Michel Fournier, Jean-Claude Galey, Kathleen Gibson, Katrin Hansing, Wendy James, Steven Lukes, Dominique Lussier, Vernon Reynolds, Nathan Schlanger, Loïc Wacquant, Willie Watts Miller. Institutionally, I am indebted at Oxford to the Institute of Social and Cultural Anthropology and to Wolfson College.

ABBREVIATIONS

Bibliographic

DOL	Durkheim 1893 (although the abbreviation is anglicised, page references are to the French text)
EF	Durkheim 1912 (same qualification)
PC	Durkheim and Mauss 1903
M	Mauss 1989 (orig. 1947)
I, II, III	Mauss 1968–69 (i.e., the volume numbers)

Other

IE	Indo-European
F1, F2, F3	First, second and third 'function' in Indo-European ideology, as most fully defined by Dumézil (1958: 18–19)
F4+, F4–	The two aspects of the fourth function

INTRODUCTION

Aims

In the physical sciences work of historical interest is not too hard to distinguish from work of current interest, that is, from work that seems to contain the promise of future advances. Naturally, the divide is not sharp and opinions differ as to exactly when the writings of a leading figure become dated and drop off the reading list into the maw of history: a couple of decades perhaps in some disciplines, even less in the disciplines that are moving fastest. In the humanities the relation between past and present is quite different. A theologian can easily turn back to Augustine or Paul, or a philosopher to Aristotle, not from an interest in disciplinary history, but with the aim of using them as starting points for new ideas.

In their use of the past, as in other ways, the social sciences stand between the sciences and the arts. Sociocultural anthropology – the attempt to come to terms intellectually with sociocultural difference – has a long prehistory, but as a sustained collective endeavour it goes back only about a century and a half. Marcel Mauss (1872–1950) is a figure from the middle third of the discipline's history, but as one of his students said not long ago, the possibilities for exploiting his formulations have doubtless not yet been exhausted (Paulme 1989: viii).

In part this is a book about what Mauss thought on various topics – Contributions to the understanding of Mauss's anthropology, as it were. Such an understanding presents certain challenges. Within the Anglophone world one of these has of course simply been the French language. Many of the more substantial essays of Mauss have now had English translations, and more are to come, but the reliability of the translations is variable, and in any case we can hardly expect translations of the whole œuvre. Moreover, Mauss's style, especially in his later years, sometimes presents a challenge even to those who read a good deal of academic French. The major problem, however, is the fragmented nature of the writing. There are no single-author books, rather a jungle of texts of varying lengths, some quite short, many unfinished, and many others presented merely as sketches or preliminary studies; one whole volume consists of unelaborated lecture notes. As Tarot puts it (1996: 143), the uncompleted quality of the œuvre (*cet insurmontable inachèvement*) is 'almost systematic'. Much work is needed before we can hope for satisfactory global assessments of Mauss's intellectual position and contribution.

Few doubt that Mauss's contribution was an important one, both as a teacher and writer. Although he lost one generation of students in the First World War, his teaching dominated interwar Parisian anthropology and affected a whole generation. His influence on Lévi-Strauss and Dumont is well known, and through them he affected structuralism and the mainstream international development of anthropology. However, increasingly it is being realised that he was also an important influence in the earlier period. In 1896 he collaborated with his uncle, Durkheim, on the statistical work for Durkheim's *Suicide*, and the flow of ideas was not only from the older man to the younger. Durkheim's *Elementary forms of religious life*, that foundational classic in the sociology of religion, owes much to his nephew.

As for the writings, there is no need to assemble the laudatory judgements of those who have commented on Mauss's special combination of breadth of knowledge and sudden profound insights. Already around 1950 in France he was a more fashionable figure than Durkheim, and although the uncle seems now to be re-established in the pantheon of the social sciences, there are some who think this pantheon needs reassessment. 'At least because of the richness and originality of the content, if not because of systematic power and scale, the work of Mauss ought to earn him the topmost steps on the podium of the social sciences' (Caillé 1996: 182).

Some of the essays below, especially Chapters 1 and 5, are primarily about Mauss's ideas, but overall my aim is less to understand a leading anthropologist from the first half of the twentieth century than to use his work as a starting point for exploring new ideas and new materials. Two main directions of exploration are essayed. One relates to palaeoanthropology (Chapters 3 and 4), and concerns the simplest and earliest forms of human society, while the other relates rather to the Indo-European world as defined by linguists (Chapters 2, 6 and 7), and concerns cultural comparativism within the framework they provide. The former, focusing on social relations and inclining more towards the sciences, belongs clearly to the social anthropology tradition. The latter, more a matter of interpretation and history of ideas, inclines more towards cultural anthropology. Although I do not regard the distinction as a fundamental one, it has often been used to contrast the dominant anthropological tradition in Britain (more social) with that in the United States (more cultural).

Mauss

How did Mauss acquire his ability to stimulate and inspire those who once knew him and those who now read him? Evidently, part of the answer lies in his personal qualities and assets, above all in the extraordinary erudition he acquired by means of the 'fabulous memory' and 'indefatigable intellectual curiosity' mentioned by Lévi-Strauss (1947: 535). Not many people would even aspire to participate actively, as Mauss did, in learned societies devoted respectively to anthropology, psychology, philosophy and sociology (Karady 1968: x). Of course, a broad education gave him a good start. As was normal at the time, his schooling in the Vosges made him familiar with the classical languages and cultures, and at university in Bordeaux and Paris he ranged widely. He studied law, philosophy (he contemplated a thesis on Spinoza), social geography, statistics, museology and above all, sociology of religion.

Even so, not every polymath is a Mauss. The crucial factor was surely his uncle. Mauss's mother had entrusted the tertiary education of her son to Durkheim, who took the responsibility seriously. Austere and self-disciplined to a degree, Durkheim was a stern mentor to the more easy-going youth. So glibly dismissed in numberless undergraduate essays, Durkheim was an extraordinary figure. On the one hand he had a systematic intellectual vision of the *sociologie* that he wanted to found. It was to be a whole, well-organised empirical science covering all kinds of social phenomena (not just the 'sociology' of our contemporary academe); and these phenomena themselves were to be carefully defined, lying as they did between the excessive particularity of the facts handled by historians and the lofty generalisations bandied about by philosophers. On the other hand, he possessed the drive and practical sense required to institutionalise his vision, partly via his own writings, but then, increasingly, by running the collaborative enterprise represented by the *Année sociologique* journal, which he founded in 1898. In directing Mauss's education he was trying to produce an ideal collaborator in this enterprise.

More specifically, Durkheim thought that the sociology of religion was inadequately developed, and in 1894/95, partly with Mauss in mind, he delivered a course of lectures on the subject. This course stimulated what Durkheim later called his 'revelation', which concerned the central role of religion in social life, and how to treat it theoretically (e.g., Steiner 1994: 21–25). The next year Mauss prepared for his contribution to this area of knowledge by beginning the philological studies that would give him access to the texts of Hinduism, Buddhism, Zoroastrianism and Judaism.

Mauss gained enormously from contact with Durkheim. The benefits included a modicum of discipline (under which admittedly he often chafed), a theoretical paradigm, which he inflected in his own way (a whole topic in itself), and encouragement to specialise in religion, which accorded with his own inclinations. But this is not the essence. What he really gained from Durkheim, I think, was the impetus, the intellectual energy, courage and confidence of a pioneer. He found himself working in what was virtually a new discipline, and expanding it so as to cover both the ancient civilisations and the radically new materials pouring in from ethnographers all over the world; and he was doing so in the context of a collectivity that was almost effervescent in Durkheim's sense. Creative intellectual work is always exciting, but not many of us can look back on a period such as Mauss describes. When he began collaborating with his friend Hubert, the two of them were in a state of enthusiasm or exhilaration bordering on madness ('nous avons été comme un peu fous', 1996: 231). The enduring freshness of Mauss's work must owe something to the social and historical context in which it was begun. It is a context that would be difficult to recreate in a globalising world whose ethnographic map is so much better known, and at a time when the various social sciences have become so much more routinised.

Any reader of *The Gift* senses the range of Mauss's erudition, and nowadays, when virtually all sociocultural anthropologists are regional specialists, it is interesting to look at the topics on which he lectured. The information on 79 of the lecture courses he gave from 1900 onwards is summarised in Appendix 1, but following is a list of the number of courses he devoted to different parts of the world. As some courses treated more than one region, the exact totals are not very meaningful, but they indicate his range and preferences.

1. Aboriginal Australia: 17 courses between 1902 and 1932, focusing above all on prayer. This was to have been the topic of his thesis (originally that of the first of its two projected volumes). To see the depth and critical quality of his knowledge of the literature it is well worth reading his essay on Australian magicians (04, II: 319 ff.).

2. Polynesia: 14 courses, two of them early (1907, 1910), but most of them in the 1930s. Polynesian cosmology became a favourite subject towards the end of his career.

3. Melanesia: 10 courses. An enduring interest spread between 1903 and 1931. Two courses focused on the work of Malinowski.[1]

4. Eskimos: 2 early courses. Native North Americans: 7 courses, mostly in connection with potlatch festivals, but at the end of his career he became particularly curious about the cosmological aspect of their games.

5. Africa: 9 courses between 1907 and 1932, mainly about West Africa. He became particularly interested in the Ashanti.

6. Germanic civilisation: 6 courses in the 1930s, essentially archaeological and historical.
7. Northeast Asia: 5 courses, all in the 1930s.
8. Indology: $2\frac{1}{2}$ courses as temporary lecturer at the Ecole Pratique des Hautes Etudes, before he was appointed there to lecture on 'the history of religions of non-civilised peoples'.
9. Not specifically regional: 6 courses.

It is noticeable that after 1901 the only literate civilisation on which he lectured was the Germanic world, when he was editing the work of Hubert. Thus none of his courses focused on tribal peoples within the sphere of Islam, China or even India, in spite of his knowledge of the subcontinent. His neglect of South America was presumably due to the poverty of the ethnography then available on that region, since he was certainly interested in envisaging the Pacific and its rim as a single cultural field. Of course, his writings show how far his interests ranged beyond those topics on which he lectured.

Sources, primary and secondary

Most of Mauss's work can be found in the following six volumes, which are described more fully in James and Allen (1998).

1. 1947. *Manuel d'ethnographie* (abbreviated hereafter as *M*). Mauss's lecture notes for his course at the Institut d'Ethnologie, edited by Denise Paulme. The course was given annually from 1926 to 1939, but towards the end of this period, with a view to publication, Mauss filled out the sections on technology and aesthetics (1935/36), juridical phenomena (1936/37), and religious phenomena (1937/38). Had he revised the work, he would no doubt have included at the end a section on 'General Sociology'. This book has often been neglected by writers on Mauss.
2. 1950. *Sociologie et anthropologie (SA)*. Six substantial essays, introduced by Lévi-Strauss. A seventh essay, that on the Eskimos, was appended in the third and subsequent editions.
3–5. 1968–69. *Œuvres*, 3 volumes, each of 600–700 pages, with a useful introduction by V. Karady. The texts are organised thematically, not chronologically, and include most of Mauss's longer book reviews. Texts are sometimes split so that (to take an extreme example) different parts of Mauss's 1901 Inaugural are to be found in each of the three volumes.
6. 1997. *Ecrits politiques*. Mauss himself distinguished sharply between his scientific and political writings, and I have scarcely drawn on the latter.

Mauss's intellectual self-portrait, an important document which I have used frequently, dates from 1930 but was first published in 1978. I have usually cited the French version in Berthoud and Busino (1996), or the translation in James and Allen (1998).

For the secondary literature on Mauss a good starting point is Berthoud and Busino (1996), with its bibliography by Moira Laffran-chini. Some other recent books are mentioned in James and Allen's 1998 volume. Fournier's biography is fascinating for a student of Mauss, but it is more the biography of an intellectual than an intellectual biography. One of the surprises to emerge is Mauss's attitude towards being a soldier during the Great War: 'I am as little as possible made for an intellectual life'; 'I was made for this and not at all for sociology'; 'Better the war than the *Année*' (Fournier 1994: 374). The background to such statements is clarified by reading Durkheim's letters to Mauss (1998). Although the two men were undoubtedly deeply attached to each other, again and again Durkheim had to reproach his nephew – for missing review deadlines, for failing to finish his thesis, for carelessness in addressing letters, for an unconventional personal life (by the standards of the day), for financial irresponsibility. Curiously, however, my own respect for his overall intellectual achievement and my liking for the man himself was, if anything, enhanced by this insight into his human failures and his openness to extra-academic experience.

If Mauss's relationship with his uncle was something of a problem for himself, it is also a problem for the analyst. How far to treat the two bodies of work as distinct, and in so far as they are distinct, what to make of the relation between them, is a delicate matter. A similar problem applies to the secondary literature. A whole tradition has grown up of commentary on Durkheim, parallel to that on Marx and Weber, and no doubt the ideally equipped student of Mauss should master not only the copious work of the uncle himself but also the even more copious work of the commentators, who are often quite separate from the Maussian commentators.

My own approach is far more limited. The great mass of serious literature on Durkheim, and much of that on Mauss is by non-anthropologists. In the main it is by sociologists in the modern sense of the term, or by philosophers (epistemologists, historians of ideas, or the like), whose lack of familiarity with sociocultural anthropology is often patent. Potentially, an anthropologist can contribute new points of view. But I would not claim to represent anthropology in general: my limits will soon become clear. Only here and there have I consulted the primary literature from which Mauss drew the facts in which he revelled, and I make few attempts to comment on his work as a whole. It is more a matter of picking up and trying to develop particular

Maussian themes or insights that happen to have struck me. A Maussian approach to Mauss perhaps, more than a Durkheimian one?

The chapters

All but the last of my seven chapters have appeared elsewhere. Though this was not the only option considered, I have retained the order in which they were written, and have edited them only lightly. I have standardised references, occasionally altered wording to improve clarity, and made a few minor corrections and additions. Contextualisation and commentary have been collected mainly in this introduction, rather than being dispersed throughout the book in the form of separate introductions or postscripts to each chapter. I have not tried to eliminate every repetition by inserting cross-references between chapters, partly because the reader may benefit from meeting similar points in different contexts, and partly because self-contained chapters are often convenient for teachers. Translations from the French are essentially my own. Where they exist, I have sometimes consulted published translations, though without acknowledgement and without necessarily following them.

Chapter 1

This chapter grew from my general interest in Mauss, combined with a particular admiration for his 1938 essay *The Person* (to abbreviate its title). Responding to my enthusiasm, Michael Carrithers, then a Junior Research Fellow at Wolfson College, Oxford, took the initiative with other colleagues in organising a series of seminars, and this led to the book (Carrithers et al. 1985) where the chapter first appeared.

Among Mauss's essays *The Person* was mentioned by Lévi-Strauss (1947: 521), not only as having been influential on Mauss's contemporaries and on younger sociologists, but also as being one of 'three real jewels' of French socioethnographic thought (together with *The Gift* from 1925 and *Seasonal variations among the Eskimos* from 1906). However, three years later, prefacing the collection *SA*, he was more critical. The main interest of the essay lay 'less in the argument, which one might well find cursory and in places negligent, than in the tendency it shows to extend to the diachronic order the technique of permutations which *The Gift* conceived as a function of synchronic phenomena'. This judgement reflects the hostility towards evolutionary and world-historical thinking that was so characteristic of the period and that still survives in parts of British social anthropology, reinforced by postmodern doubts about 'Grand Narratives'. Chapter 1 therefore starts with a defence of this aspect of Mauss's thought – a theme that will recur in later chapters.

The core of the chapter is an attempt to fill out the argument that Lévi-Strauss condemned and that is certainly not easy reading. One basic problem that continues to worry me is what to make of Mauss's statement that his essay is confined to the domain of *droit et morale*, law and morality. This implies that, contrary to what one might think, it does not fall under the rubric of religion. Even so, the statement is not absolutely true – witness the important references to totemism and religious festivals in the first part, and to Christianity and the sacred character of the human person in the second. Perhaps it should be taken merely as an indication of the intended emphasis. The essay was to be more about the person as bearer of rights and duties than about the person in relation to the sacred, about pneumatology or the theory of the soul. But perhaps a second explanation is also relevant. Mauss only explicitly connects 'the sacred character of the human person' with Kant, but his use of the phrase in his penultimate paragraph cannot fail to recall Durkheim's notion of a religion of humanity or cult of the person. As Durkheim put it in 1898, 'just as each of us incarnates something of humanity, so each individual mind has within it something of the divine, and thereby finds itself marked by a characteristic which renders it sacred and inviolable to others' (Durkheim 1994: 67). However, Durkheim was writing, not about religion as such, but as an opponent of the anti-Dreyfusards in the context of the great politico-legal scandal that was rocking France at the time. This may go some way towards explaining Mauss's emphasis on *droit et morale*. In addition, however, one might wonder whether the remark was oriented towards the British audience on the occasion of the 1938 Huxley Memorial Lecture: he once equated the French legal-moral rubric with 'what the Anglo-Saxons call "social anthropology"' (*M*: 135).

A broader question raised by Mauss's phrase is the place of religion in his general outlook. Durkheim, the son of a rabbi, although not an adherent of any formal religion, was in a sense a profoundly religious man, who surely believed in the religion of humanity that he formulated, in 'societism' as Prades calls it (1987: 218). In respecting the power of sacred beings, humanity was recognising a reality, albeit in symbolic form – the reality of the power exerted by society, and since humans would always belong to societies, the sacred could never entirely disappear. Indeed, in spite of difficulties of definition, there is much to be said in support of the Durkheimian nexus 'duty-God-love-solidarity-society-totality'. For one thing, it provides the only moderately clear middle ground between, on the one hand, the supernaturalism of the contending faiths, and on the other the potential amoralism of neo-Darwinian or other attempts at a complete elimination of the sacred. Moreover, as Prades shows (1987: 147 ff., 252 ff.), criticisms by well-known figures such as Stanner or Evans-Pritchard can be answered. Durkheim's position remains tenable, and although there is scope for a fuller study of the point, *The Person* can probably be read as an endorsement by Mauss of his uncle's general attitude towards the sacredness of the person.

Apart from Mauss's interest in world history, Chapter 1 raises several other topics that will recur below. Among these are his interest in categories and the massive long-term historical processes of homogenisation within them; in the aesthetic domain and in material culture; in festivals and 'total social facts'; in primitive classifications and the importance of giving due weight to the differentiations they make as well as to the assimilations; in the identification of alternate generations that occurs when a grandparent transmits name and soul to a grandchild. I also refer briefly to some of his departures from the views of his uncle.

Chapter 2

Written in the early 1990s, this is a paper about the 1903 essay by Durkheim and Mauss on 'primitive classification'. The phenomenon in question will be familiar to some readers from European history of ideas. An instance is provided by the doctrines of Galen (second century AD), which remained popular throughout the Middles Ages, and even later (e.g. Palmer 1998).

> (Galenic theory) locked man's psychology into the cosmos, for the four humours correspond to four elements and four planets, as follows:
>
>   Sanguine – Air – Jupiter
>   Choleric – Fire – Mars
>   Phlegmatic – Water – Moon
>   Melancholy – Earth – Saturn
>
> The theory was bound up with astrology. If Saturn dominated in a horoscope, the person concerned would be inclined to melancholy; if Jupiter, the outlook would be more hopeful, and so on. (Yates 1979: 51)

Of course, in many contexts one finds more than three quaternities, for instance four colours are often linked with the humours (cf. Allen 1998f). However, this particular schema has the advantage of simplicity and serves to raise one of the main themes of the chapter. The problem is how to characterise such schemata, to identify their logic. It is clear at once that the schema has two distinct 'dimensions'. In one dimension the four items of each quaternity unroll one after the other, and in the other each item of one quaternity is linked with one item from each of the other quaternities. Yates has chosen to depict the first dimension vertically, by putting each quaternity in a column, and the second dimension horizontally, but I prefer the reverse layout. One reason for this preference, among several, is that if there were many more than three quaternities to be shown, say a dozen, it would be easier to show them in columns than in rows. But whichever option one follows for the display, two dimensions are needed.

Moreover, the two dimensions have quite different properties. A quick way to see this is to ask of a column or row what sort of entity it contains. Yates's leftmost column contains humours – no problem there. But what sort of entity is contained in her top row? No obvious label comes to mind. The entities that are linked to the sanguine humour? Entities associated with Jupiter? Similarly, the relations that link one humour with another are different from those that link a humour with an element and a planet. In attempting to think clearly about these differences, I draw on Saussure's opposition between syntagmatic and paradigmatic relations in language. There are certainly some similarities between the two cases, as well as differences, but it is for the reader to judge whether the Saussurean terminology is really helpful.

In some contexts, schemata of the sort discussed are complicated by what I call a third dimension. Sometimes, a quaternity will consist not of a whole named domain divided into four, but of a domain first divided into two, each half then being bisected. This brings out a third type of relation, that between different taxonomic levels. Such taxonomies can conveniently be shown by branching diagrams, often with the whole at the top and the smallest units at the bottom, though of course the orientation on the page is ultimately trivial. This third, or hierarchical, dimension potentially gives a pattern to the list of entities making up a domain, and that pattern may or may not be carried through to the other domains linked with the patterned one.

A second theme of the chapter is the argument of Durkheim and Mauss in *Primitive Classification*. I attempt to clarify this and to defend it against criticisms made by its English translator. But for the later chapters of the book, the most important theme is the connection between this argument and Indo-European comparativism as practised by Georges Dumézil. The connection comes in two forms. On the one hand, I argue for a continuity of ideas running from the 1903 essay via the Sinologist Granet to Dumézil's breakthrough in 1938. On the other, I argue that, although Dumézil does not refer to *PC*, his analyses complement that work by bringing to light a fourth type of primitive classification to add to the three on which Durkheim and Mauss concentrated. I emphasise the similarities of the fourth type to the others, rather than its differences from them, and barely allude to the way in which I think Dumézil's theory needs elaboration. In spite of the risk of circularity, I suggest that the parallel between *PC* and Dumézil's work strengthens both of them. It brings the 'primitives' of 1903 closer to Europe, and it makes the Indo-Europeans more 'anthropological'.

Chapters 3 and 4

Chapter 3 was first presented at the ASA Decennial Conference in Oxford in 1993, at a session commemorating the centenary of the publication of Durkheim's *Division of labour* and organised by the British Centre for Durkheimian Studies. Chapter 4 was given at a conference organised by the Centre in Oxford in 1995 and devoted to Durkheim's *Elementary Forms*. They are treated together here because, in spite of their different starting points, they converge on the topic of kinship and social structure, and there is even some overlap between them. This field is often regarded as the most difficult and technical area of social anthropology (and tends to be unpopular with students of the subject for that reason), so it may be useful to see the same issues approached from different directions.

I doubt whether the subject is intrinsically or absolutely difficult, as might be a mathematical argument or a chess problem. I see two factors in the reputed difficulty. The basic problem concerns cultural relativity. It is easy to see that what is sacred, or authoritative, or valuable, or beautiful, varies with cultures but it is not so obvious that the same applies to the domain of kinship and marriage. One expects cultural variability as regards the ritual and legal status of members of the family, and perhaps even as regards rules of incest, but it is easy to assume that in other respects the facts of biology provide a universal basis for this domain of social life. In one sense they do (if one ignores recent advances in reproductive medicine); even animals have parents and children, siblings and mates or partners (if not spouses). But in another sense, humanity, and especially tribal societies, have taken the biology and used it to weave structures and entities such as seldom come the way of non-anthropological Westerners. 'Elementary structures of kinship', as Lévi-Strauss called them, provide configurations of the domain that differ from the familiar 'complex' ones in ways that are entirely objective – they would show up in genealogical records.

To talk about such configurations just a few technical terms are needed, such as 'moiety', 'section' and 'clan'. These terms are probably best introduced, as is done here, by starting not from the familiar nuclear family and working outwards, but from the theoretical notion of a bounded and enduring horde, into which rules of marriage and recruitment are introduced so as to produce the smaller units. As in *PC*, one needs to take account of both 'horizontal' and 'vertical' dimensions, since kinship covers the social relations involved not only in producing new generations (marriage) but also in incorporating them into society (recruitment).

A second major factor in the reputed difficulty of the field is the complexity of the literature. In part, this results from the arguments and misunderstandings of the specialists. Such arguments have helped me towards whatever clarity I have achieved, but they are barely discussed here since they did not seem sufficiently important for the questions I was asking. Admittedly, some of the complexity is also intrinsic to those attested systems that stand typologically, and no doubt world-historically, around the half-way point in the scale leading from the simplest logical possibilities to the Western system. Fortunately, though, such intermediate systems are not relevant here.

Chapter 3 focuses on Durkheim's notion of tribal solidarity, or rather on Mauss's equivalent notion of cohesion. Mauss saw this cohesion as resulting from cross-cutting identities, and it requires only a slight tidying up of his ideas to produce a model of the utmost formal simplicity, in which two cross-cutting dichotomies generate a third.[2] This model is proposed as an improvement on Durkheim's notion of mechanical solidarity produced by a set of juxtaposed similar clans.

Chapter 4 focuses on Durkheim's treatment of effervescence in *EF*, since that book was the subject of the conference. But it was Mauss, writing in 1906 on the Eskimos, who first elaborated on effervescence in the context of tribal societies: 'Winter is a season when the society, strongly concentrated, is in a continuous state of effervescence and hyperactivity' (*SA*: 470). His point is to contrast the continuous religious activity of the winter with the dispersed, religiously quiescent social life of the summer, and the direction of his thought is indicated by a remark attributed to the Kwakiutl of the Canadian west coast: 'In summer the sacred is below, the profane above; in winter the sacred is above, the profane below.'[3] The connection between social concentration and religion is fundamental. It is widely known that many tribal societies assemble for rituals involving dancing (hyperactivity), but apparently, in their thinking about the origins of human culture, palaeoanthropologists have largely neglected the point.

In fact Durkheim may well have been right in regarding such assemblies as the context in which humanity first experienced the forces exerted by society and began to symbolise them by sacred objects and beings, thus originating the basic notions of religion. The chapter tries to take Durkheim's argument further. Durkheim is trying to find the simplest attested religion by looking at societies with the simplest attested social structures, and indeed the totemic religion he discusses is, like many other ideologies, closely linked to the social structure (the emphasis is on totemic clans). Perhaps then we should regard the effervescent assemblies as the context for the development of *both* sorts of social phenomenon. We again need a model of the simplest possible type of social structure, which is introduced for a second time but with different imagery from that used in Chapter 3.

In exploring this idea Chapter 4 will seem to some excessively speculative. But all arguments about humanity's origins are speculative, and the chapter is probably no more so than most scientistic theories based solely on ecology, cognitive science or the like, which ignore great tracts of what ethnography can tell us about the importance of kinship and of ritual assemblies in tribal life.

One suggestion I make ('a fourfold idea of the sacred') is perhaps particularly Maussian. Looking back on his prewar work, Mauss saw it as excessively influenced by the simple binary opposition between sacred and profane, which Hertz had correlated with right and left (33, II: 147): 'but once what dominates [the ideology] is a complex of positions, powers and purities all together – not that of power without purity or power without position – then the simple right-left division is used as one element in the whole'. Though he does not mention the Zuñi, his reference earlier in the same paragraph to 'seven positions in the interior of a sort of sphere' suggests that the 'positions' in his complex are cardinal points, with which different qualities (such as power or purity or types of them) are associated. In any case, he is suggesting that we need a concept of the sacred as multiple or plural. A unitary sacred, like a unified concept of space or of relatives, or like a high god replacing a polytheism, could (among other possibilities) result from homogenisation.

Although my main suggestion is that holistic kinship systems originated in effervescent assemblies, one spin-off is the hypothesis that initiation rituals are to child exchange what weddings are to spouse exchange, or rather that this was the case originally. Certainly child exchange in the specified sense has been relatively neglected in anthropology. I stumbled upon the idea by combining Mauss's remarks on name/soul transmission between alternate generations with Lévi-Strauss's idea of the exchange of women, which he derived from Mauss's *The Gift*.

The next Maussian paper I wrote (Allen 1998e) would have fitted perfectly well in this volume had it not appeared in a previous volume of the same series from the same publisher. Although it is not reprinted here, its relevance justifies a brief summary. It starts by trying to recover as many as possible of the ideas that Mauss would have put into the two- or three-volume work that he had planned to write with Hubert on the category of substance. The pair were planning to relate substance to cosmogony, food, femaleness and number, and also to compare ancient Greece and Vedic India. The major part of the paper then moves to Indo-European comparativism and uses four-function theory, as distinct from Dumézil's trifunctionalism, to analyse the Hindu philosophy of Sāṃkhya, which gives an account of the substance of the cosmos.

Chapter 5

This paper was originally written for a conference on Mauss held in the Collège de France and the Maison des Sciences de l'Homme in 1997, and organised by Marcel Fournier. It represents the start of a shift in my own view of Mauss: beginning with the customary observations on Mauss's avoidance of explicit system-building, it moves towards the view of him in Chapter 6 as someone whose thought was a good deal more systematic or orderly than it has appeared to be.

The main point of this chapter is the suggestion that *The Gift* was a preliminary study towards a sociological understanding of Aristotle's category of relation. It remains somewhat puzzling that Mauss never stated this, and indeed the whole subject of the categories is surrounded by epistemological and other puzzles. However, it is also a subject that could not be avoided by anyone attempting a thorough treatment of the thought of either Durkheim or Mauss.

When introducing the categories in *EF*, Durkheim famously describes them as ideas so fundamental that apparently human thought cannot do without them; 'they seem to us almost inseparable from the normal functioning of the mind' (*EF*: 13). Fascinated as he was by questions of morality, one might then wonder what links Durkheim, or someone developing his thought, would make between the traditional set of categories and ideas of right and wrong. *The Gift* provides one pointer towards an answer. It is largely about the three obligations – to give, to receive, to return – and the facts it assembles are intended to contribute to 'a general theory of obligation' (25, *SA*: 160–61). It thus links with the previous chapter, since it is arguable that the most fundamental obligations, humanity's first rules, related to kinship and to the giving of life to new generations.

Chapter 6

This was written on the request of Loïc Wacquant for the journal *Body and Society*. If Allen (1998e) raised the idea of Mauss the Indo-European comparativist, Chapter 6 looks at Mauss the lover of classifications. He saw himself primarily as a lover of facts, 'a positivist, believing only in facts'; if he practised theory, it was because it could help us to observe, record and reclassify facts (1996: 225). But the theory, and the classifications it produced, were important to him and are often mentioned or implied in his writings. Thus I do not altogether agree with Paulme's characterisation of the *Manuel* as 'dry, lacking in general ideas, precise, unhesitating' (1989: iii). The adjectives can stand, but Mauss's organisation of the facts and instructions amounts to a 'general idea' of great scope. His 'plan for the study of a society' (*M*: 14) is a theory about what sorts of social phenomena make up social life. Admittedly, he later says that ethnographers 'will have to train themselves systematically to break down all the divisions that I am here expounding from a didactic standpoint. [Social] things are not divided up any more than a living being is divided up. We are beings who are all of one piece [*formons bloc*], collectively and individually' (*M*: 235). Nevertheless, his classifications were more to him than mere pedagogic aids. I doubt whether he ever lost the belief that it was possible to set up 'natural' classes of facts (04, *SA*: 138), i.e., classes that nature itself separated.

Sometimes Mauss explicitly borrowed ideas from the cultures that he studied (*mana* from the Melanesians, *hau* in *The Gift* from the Maori), and he sometimes did the same with classifications. He showed a particular regard for the Hindus, and turned to them several times for classifications: of sacrifices into regular and occasional (99, I: 206–7); of sources of magic power in Australia (14, II: 327); and of cults into domestic and public (*M*: 214). But these were classifications useful to the analyst in organising facts from quite narrow domains within the sphere of religion. The classification of social facts in general is a different matter.

For the editors of *L'Année sociologique* such classification was an important matter, and the rubrics of the journal were adjusted from time to time, with or without published discussion. No doubt, interesting work could be done on the proximate origins of the overall scheme that they followed. However, one of the main arguments of the chapter is that, ultimately, their classification can be traced back to the five-fold Indo-European form of primitive classification. In organising the *Manuel* in the way he did, Mauss was, while perhaps only half realising it, continuing a very old pattern of thought.

To some readers Indo-European cultural comparativism may seem a remote and obscure branch of research, most unlikely to be relevant to understanding a twentieth-century anthropologist. Some established academics too, doubt whether it is a feasible undertaking, even for much earlier periods. But research continues, and the general outcome has been to show the pervasiveness and endurance of bits and pieces of the old ideology over surprisingly wide stretches of space and time. Dismissive judgements from senior figures, or junior ones for that matter, are not necessarily well-founded, and often reflect excessive respect for traditional disciplinary boundaries. Certainly Mauss was well aware of the metaphysical axis of his *Manuel*; 'The whole course here published sets off from the study of material phenomena to end up in the study of ideal phenomena' (*M*: 203). This comes at the start

of the final chapter, which is on religion, while Chapter 6, on economics, opens: 'Of all moral phenomena, economic ones are those that
remain the most engaged in matter' (*M*: 123). But few will jib at supposing that the scale leading upwards from matter to ideality and the
divine goes back to Plato; and as the end of Chapter 6 argues, following other IE comparativists, aspects of Plato's thought show the characteristic IE fivefold pattern. No doubt, the social sciences generally
tend to exaggerate the novelty of their propositions.

Perhaps too, this area of research will one day move closer to common knowledge. A recent novel by Salman Rushdie includes a Parsi
character who 'was particularly drawn to the so-called tripartite theory of Dumézil'.

> One day, however, Sir Darius took off his half-rimmed spectacles, banged
> his fist on the table and shouted: 'It isn't enough.'. . .
>   'Three functions aren't enough,' he said feverishly. 'There must be a
> fourth.'
>   'Can't be,' said Methwold. 'Those three concepts of old Georges's [reli-
> gious sovereignty, physical force and fertility] fill out the insides of the
> whole social picture.'
>   'Yes,' said Sir Darius. 'But what about *outsideness*? What about all that
> which is beyond the pale, above the fray, beneath notice?' (Rushdie 1999:
> 42)[4]

Chapter 7

The original intention with this paper was to attempt for the category
of cause what other papers had attempted for the categories of person,
class, substance and relation. However, I found this difficult, and
increasingly moved towards an issue adumbrated in a discussion of
the pervasiveness of the four-function ideology in Hinduism: 'A distinction is needed between religion as pervading the whole ideology
and religion as concentrated within the first function' (Allen 1999b:
256). The thrust of the paper therefore, is to emphasise distinctions
within our notion of religion.

It was partly because of such distinctions that the Durkheimians
avoided the reification lurking in the word 'religion', and preferred to
talk of *faits religieux*, religious facts or phenomena. Together with
Durkheim and Hubert, Mauss constituted what analysts call the
'innermost circle' of the *Année* team (Steiner 1994: 11), and they all
shared this view. Thus, when he tried to define religious phenomena in
1899, Durkheim emphasised that every society contained some such
facts that were not integrated into systems, i.e., that constituted folklore (1994: 74). In his introduction to a compendium of comparative
religion, Hubert echoes Durkheim's arguments, adding that 'the science of religion must study religious facts before studying religion, just

as biology must study biological facts before studying life' (1904: xx). Commenting on this text, Mauss says that in it Hubert 'expounds ideas that are to such an extent shared between us, and does so in a form that is so profoundly familiar to me, that I should be a poor critic of them' (05, I: 46).

Apart from folklore, the other major class of religious phenomena was magic, but it did not follow necessarily that what was left when these two compartments were hived off constituted a homogeneous rubric of religion in the strict sense. Mauss himself certainly recognised a further division that he called divination, but divination in turn was very closely related to cosmology. There is a potential divide here, which could be important for the study of religion – a field which is so often conceived of as defined by unitary concepts such as the sacred or the holy.

In exploring this topic the chapter takes a tip from Mauss's criticism of the prewar work by himself and Hertz. Responding to a paper by Granet, he said: 'The great effort that we made on the side of the study of ritual lacks balance because we did not make the corresponding effort on mythology' (33, II: 146). In *Année* parlance, *mythologie* covered belief systems as well as mythic narratives, and accordingly, in looking at the classification of religious phenomena, the chapter concentrates both on the Indo-European ideology and its expression in the mythology of the *Mahābhārata*. It is interesting that, in the same text, Mauss goes on to talk of three things: the category of space, which was being studied by the Celticist Czarnowski, divination, and then cosmologies, which he implicitly links to the cardinal points. As it happens, the first recognition of the fivefold structure of the Indo-European ideology was due to Celticists working on the origin myths and, especially, on the sacred geography of early Ireland (Rees and Rees 1961: 118–39).

Notes

1. While admiring Malinowski's ethnography, Mauss commented on his 'theoretical weakness and total lack of erudition' (letter to Radcliffe Brown in 1935, Fournier 1994: 637).
2. One could no doubt arrive at the same ideas by starting from Granet (1939), or perhaps from Hocart, or others, but Granet at least was influenced by Mauss.
3. In his translation Fox (1979: 121) correctly points out that here Mauss has taken liberties with the precise wording of the ethnographer (Boas).
4. The author kindly informs me that he became aware of four-function theory via Baldick (1994).

Chapter 1

The category of the person:
a reading of Mauss's last essay

The Person, as I shall call it,[1] can stimulate exploration of particular cultures in all sorts of ways, and the more the better. However, there is also much room for reflection simply on the purpose of Mauss's paper as he saw it and on its place within his thought. As it stands, it has a compressed and allusive quality that accounts for part of its charm, but at the same time moves it away from most academic prose in the direction of fine literature, almost poetry (cf. Dumont 1972: 18). The full meaning scarcely emerges unless it is read in the light of the rest of his work. Conversely, the essay clarifies, almost epitomises, a lifetime's thinking by one of the great minds of social anthropology. Although there have been a number of attempts to express what is essential in Mauss's contribution to the subject, none of them takes *The Person* as starting point.[2]

I shall not consider the general theoretical problems of assessing someone's 'thought', but regarding Mauss specifically it needs to be said that much of his early work was published jointly with other members of the *Année* school. The difficult problem of isolating his own contribution will be touched on only in passing. Indeed, beyond a certain point such a separation would be meaningless, as is clear from the important summary of his academic activity (1979), which he prepared (without false modesty) in connection with his candidature for the Collège de France.

Evolutionism

The structure of *The Person* is clear. Apart from the introduction and conclusion, the paper consists of an ethnographic section dealing with tribal societies and a historical section dealing with Europe, the latter being introduced in brief paragraphs on the ancient oriental civilisations. The relationship between the two main sections is frankly evolutionary: tribal societies observed and described within the last century are adduced as representing a type of society which preceded the Greco-Roman and the other historical civilisations. Thus I begin by considering Mauss's evolutionism, an aspect of his thought that is often dismissed as outmoded even by people who admire and use other aspects of his work. He himself was of course aware of contrary trends in the subject, but refused to join in the 'scalp dance' over the collapse of evolutionism (27, III: 287).

The label 'evolutionist' is an unhappy one since it covers such a variety of positions. Surprisingly often, it is still understood as connoting the speculations, dogmatism and complacency of nineteenth-century theorists with their now wholly discarded notions of 'primitive promiscuity', 'primitive matriarchy' and the like. Perhaps it would be better to talk rather of Mauss's world-historical awareness, i.e., his habit of assessing particular cultures or social phenomena against the history of humanity as a whole. Such assessments more or less necessitate a concept of types of society ranging from primitive to modern, and this forms a constant background to Mauss's work. In *The Person,* as often, the typology is largely implicit, but even here his assumptions are apparent in the three uses of the word 'primitive' in the tribal half of the essay. Sometimes he is explicit. 'One can classify societies into four great groups', he writes in 1920 (III: 580), and goes on to offer a straightforward evolutionary typology of political structures. In the simplest type (segmentary or polysegmentary), the whole society is divided into totemic clans, and central authority is non-existent.

In most contexts, however, Mauss emphatically rejected the notion of an undifferentiated tribal stage in human history. In his Inaugural Lecture (02, II: 231–32), and repeatedly thereafter (e.g., 33, II: 233), he consistently presented Australian aboriginal societies as the most primitive that were accessible to history or ethnography (as distinct from prehistoric archaeology). Unfortunately the even more primitive Tasmanians (Aurignacians, as he sometimes called them [*M*: 32, 216]) had been destroyed too soon to count as accessible, and it was only the Australians, as survivors from the Palaeolithic age, who could properly be termed primitive (e.g., 23, II: 128).

Whatever one thinks of this approach (and the question is not easily settled), Mauss avoided the crudity of certain styles of evolutionism. If Australian societies were primitive in type, it by no means followed that they had merely endured unchanged over the millennia (08, II: 201). The point is that they 'allow one, while supposing behind them a long history, to represent to oneself schematically the first human groupings from which the others have originated' (09, I: 420).

Although he took it as plausible that primitivity in certain respects should be accompanied by primitivity in others (ibid.: 427), he was quite clear that the history of particular societies did not necessarily follow the unilineal schemata one can construct for humanity as a whole (01, III: 152; 05, I: 164). Moreover, after the First World War he came to realise that in so vast a field premature systematisation was unprofitable (33, III: 438), and he warned the fieldworker against searching for the primitive (*M*: 205). In any case rudimentary forms were not necessarily easy to understand: they had their own type of complexity resulting from the mutual interpenetration of elements and meanings which would be distinct in more evolved forms (09, I: 396; 34, II: 149; *M*: 209).

Like his uncle, Durkheim, Mauss saw the study of the primitive as central to the sociological enterprise. In 1909, in the introduction to his thesis on prayer (which concentrated on the Australians), he put the matter clearly:

> I believe that in sociology the study of primitive forms [*formes frustes*] is, and will long remain, more interesting and more urgent, even for the understanding of contemporary phenomena, than the study of the forms that immediately preceded the latter. It is not always the phenomena closest in time that are the profound causes of the phenomena we are familiar with. (09, I: 366)

It is true that later (possibly under the influence of Granet), Mauss came to think that the prewar *Année* had neglected the older literate civilisations and overdone the primitive (27, III: 184; 295); but this was a matter of emphasis.

The argument

In *The Person* Mauss undertakes to lead us 'from Australia to our European societies', but in fact he starts not with Australia but with the 'far from primitive' North American Indians. The main reason is probably that the relevant Australian phenomena are more summary and less clear-cut ('moins net' 06, II: 138) – he often stressed the advantage of studying a social phenomenon in a society exemplifying it in an extreme form. Perhaps he also wanted to start with a society that used masks, since it is the Latin *'persona* equals mask' that bridges the two halves of the essay, and its French derivative, *personne*, that is the key word in the title. I suspect too, that he had a particular affection for the Zuñi. They were prominent in 1903 in *PC*, which (excluding book reviews) was his first substantial venture into tribal ethnographic materials, and he was still lecturing on the same people in 1940

(II: 268). Moreover, he particularly admired Cushing, a 'profound observer and *sociologue génial*' (27, III: 185) who had anticipated some of the ideas in *PC* (04, II: 311). Whatever the reasons,[3] the implication of his ordering of the paper is that so far as the category of the person is concerned, the primitiveness of the Australians in technology and in other respects makes little difference. To a first approximation, all the tribal peoples mentioned (North American, Pacific, African) share a similar notion of the person.

If we ask what exactly is the notion that is supposed to have evolved in the transition from tribal life to Mauss's contemporary Europe, we meet first a terminological problem that constantly recurs in anthropology. We have little alternative but to analyse alien cultures using vocabulary developed in our own, but the result is that terms for social phenomena become systematically ambiguous. Words like 'law', 'religion', or 'kinship' may mean (i) what they are ordinarily taken to mean in English, (ii) the nearest equivalent in some alien society or group of societies, or (iii) what is common to both usages. Thus Mauss is sometimes dealing with the contemporary idea of the person (which we wrongly believe to be innate), sometimes with its nearest equivalent in cultures remote in space or time (Zuñi, Rome), and sometimes with the deeper, more theoretical concept that gives the essay its unity. It is unfortunate that readers are left to make the distinctions themselves, but to do so greatly clarifies the argument. Modern society has a concept of the person (usage i), many tribal societies have or had a related concept (usage ii), and it is the concept in usage iii that has evolved from one to the other, and will evolve further.

Mauss was naturally aware of these distinctions: 'Our music is only one music, and yet there exists something that merits the name of "Music" . . . it is the same with all the major classes of social phenomena' (34, II: 152). Indeed in his early writings he laid considerable emphasis on preliminary definitions, both in his methodological statements (01, III: 164–66) and in his empirical studies (e.g., *Sacrifice* 99, I: 205, *Magic* 04, *SA*: 16, *Prayer* 09, I: 414), where they are regularly italicised. The object was to avoid prejudicing the investigation by some ethnocentric contemporary category or by some inappropriate would-be native category such as 'fetishism'. The concept of the person, let alone the self, is so close to one that it is apt to blur when one tries to focus on it, and it is regrettable that he did not follow his early practice of giving an explicit definition of the subject of the essay. However, I think the gap is filled by the statement that the investigation will be entirely one of 'droit et morale'. These are broad rubrics, since in the language of the *Année* the juridical includes the realm of kinship as well as politics and law, while 'morale' (*M*: 199) covers the values and general ethos of a society.[4] Nevertheless, we can specify that the essay concerns essentially the concept of the individual presupposed by or expressed in a society's dominant value system or encompassing ideology. The emphasis is on the public and institutional domain; a society's theories of the biological, psychological and metaphysical nature of humanity are relevant only in so far as they affect 'droit et morale'. Understood as I have defined it, the category of the person is necessarily present in some form, however indistinct, in any society worthy of the name. It could only be wholly absent in a 'society', presumably pre-human, that lacked values and institutions.

It might be objected that the formulation I offer lays the emphasis too much on the sociology and on the ethnographic half of the essay, too little on the philosophy and the European history. There are several answers to this. The philosophical language is in part a hangover from Durkheim's struggle to establish an academic niche for sociology, to found a discipline combining the empiricism of the natural sciences with the profundity of philosophy. The list of categories was probably little more than a convenient and suggestive device for organising the division of labour among members of the *Année* school (but compare Chapters 5 and 6). As for the philosophers, they earn their place in the essay mainly because they articulate the concepts of the person that were expressed in society more or less contemporaneously with them, that is, in the sectarian movements[5] or in the Declarations of Rights – see the treatment in *The Nation* (20, III: 592–93) of the writers and philosophers who translated into words what was already present in society. 'The sacred character of the human person' may be important intellectually in the philosophy of Kant and his followers, but it is relevant in *The Person* because it is presupposed by the social and educational ideals of a liberal democratic state. No doubt, in so far as the philosophers suppose themselves to be working *a priori*, purely by means of reasoning from first principles, they exemplify the characteristic error of non-sociologists who, unaware of the history and pre-history of the fundamental notions with which they operate, naively regard them as natural.

Mauss's fundamental commitment to a sociological approach is well illustrated by his critical attitude to his colleague, Lévy-Bruhl, whose books were widely read and of whom he wrote a warm obituary (39, III: 560). A philosopher by training and profession, Lévy-Bruhl had later turned to anthropology and attempted to specify the most general characteristics of primitive thought. As he implies at the start of *The Person*, Mauss thought this approach was too broad: Lévy-Bruhl would have done better to limit himself to studying particular categories. Elsewhere, he also criticised the philosopher's insufficient sensitivity to world history, and especially his tendency to abstract an idea from its related social institutions and milieu. For instance, Lévy-Bruhl was perfectly correct in noting that many more or less tribal societies identified an individual's name with his soul, but this was merely to *describe* the facts. 'A sociologist of the strict obedience' – Mauss means a true Durkheimian – would *understand* the belief by showing its foundation in social organisation (23, 29, II: 125–35). What Lévy-Bruhl saw as a problem in primitive cognition, a topic for psychological and philosophical consideration, Mauss saw as one social phenomenon among others, as something to be related to other aspects of the life of members of societies. He even went so far as to suggest (ibid.: 128) that a complete anthropology could replace philosophy 'since it would comprehend precisely that history of the human mind that philosophy takes for granted'. It is this aspect of Mauss's position that explains the brevity of his remarks on India. The ancient metaphysicians invented sophisticated notions of the person closer in character to modern European ideas than to tribal ones, and these even enjoyed considerable currency through religious teaching and writing. But they did not come to dominate 'droit et morale': they were submerged within the encompassing ideology of caste.

The *personnage*

The main purpose of Mauss's essay, then, is to establish a baseline notion of the person obtaining in tribal society – let us call this elementary form *the personnage* – and then to link it to contemporary notions of the person. Being embedded in beliefs and institutions of various kinds, the concept of the person is not the sort of entity that is immediately accessible.

> Just as the linguist must recover beneath the false transcriptions of an alphabet the true sounds [*phonèmes*] that were pronounced, so beneath the information of the best of the natives, Oceanian or American, the ethnographer must recover the deep phenomena, the ones which are almost unconscious, since they exist only in the collective tradition. It is these real phenomena, these *choses* [i.e., Durkheimian social facts] that we shall try to reach through the documentation. (02, III: 369)

The brief sketches of the tribes in *The Person* are miniature synchronic analyses, but since Mauss's style is suggestive rather than systematic I will attempt below to summarise and fill out the picture he presents.

1. The *personnage* is a member of a bounded tribal society. While recognising that in practice an ethnographer might find it extremely problematic to identify such a social entity (*M*: 23), Mauss there and elsewhere offered definitions of a society. The

essence is a definite group with a sense of attachment to a tract of territory and a shared 'constitution' (10, III: 377). The group will be large enough to contain at least two subgroups and several generations, and its sense of wholeness and distinctness from others will generally be expressed in a name, a belief in common origin and an aspiration to internal harmony (M: 141–42; 34, III: 306–7; 314–15). Many tribal self-appellations mean something like 'man' or 'human', outsiders being by implication non-man and *a fortiori* not *personnages*.

2. The tribe is divided into segments that may cross-cut each other (clans, age-sets, sections, etc. [31, III: 11ff.]. The prototypical *personnage* for Mauss would seem to be a member of a totemic clan. Totemism is the commonest religious system in societies where social organisation is based on clans, though it is not possible to say whether all societies have passed through a totemic phase. One should not talk of totemism unless there is a theriomorphic cult practised by clans, each of which bears an animal name, or less commonly, the name of some other natural species (05, I: 163; 06, I: 40). Mauss's later definitions also mention a belief in community of substance between the natural species and the members of the clan (or other social unit) such that both are of the same nature and possess the same virtues (M: 160–61; 218).

3. The totemic group possesses a fixed stock of names (*prénoms*) and souls, one for each *personnage*. This is another sense in which the society is closed or bounded.

4. The bearer of a name at any time is regarded as the reincarnation of the original mythical bearer. (Points 3 and 4 seem to be at the very centre of Mauss's concept.)

5. The name may have a meaning relating to the clan's ancestral totem and the associated mythological narratives. These narratives will be acted out at initiation ceremonies (M: 220–21).

6. A name is commonly taken over from a grandfather or great-great-grandfather, though there are other possibilities (Kwakiutl, Winnebago), including divination (as in Dahomey [M: 229]).

7. The bearer of a name has the right and duty at ritual gatherings to represent the original bearer and/or to be possessed by his spirit. This may involve wearing the ancestral mask. However, the identity of performer and ancestor can be symbolised in other ways, and there is no difference in principle between enduring masks and body paintings created afresh for each ritual according to a traditional pattern; in any case, masks are often burnt after one use (M: 102).

8. The ritual regularly involves dancing, an art often learned at initiation (M: 224).

9. Members of a clan are not necessarily *personnages*. This may be because they have had to retire owing to old age or are still too young, or because they are female. 'In a great number of cases women do not reincarnate'; they may 'have no soul' (*M*: 229; 156). It would seem that some clan members otherwise qualified could not be *personnages* because there would not be enough names to go round (unless there were some doubling up). This demographic difficulty seems to be the aspect of the paper that most needs touching up, even in a 'clay model' for a full study. Nor is it clear whether people who are not *personnages* are 'non-persons' in the same sense as outsiders to the society or as Roman slaves. I suppose not, and this implies the possibility of gradations of personhood.

Despite such uncertainties, one can sum up Mauss's vision as follows: a bounded society consisting of totemic clans, each clan having a fixed stock of names transmitted by recognised procedures, the bearers of a name being reincarnations of their predecessors back to mythical times and dancing out that fact at rituals.

Development of Mauss's ideas

The idea is one that Mauss had been developing for a very long time. Already in 1902 (I: 490) he was describing magico-religious birth among the Australian Arunta as a 'truly elementary phenomenon, explanatory of numerous customs', for instance of the frequent practice of recognising a child as some particular ancestor and giving him the latter's name. By 1906 the essentials were well established:

> There exists an enormous group of societies, Negro, Malayo-Polynesian, Amerindian (Sioux, Algonquin, Iroquois, Pueblo, North-Western), Eskimo, Australian, where the system of reincarnation of the deceased and inheritance of the name within the family or clan is the rule. The individual is born with his name and his social functions . . . The number of individuals, names, souls and roles is limited in the clan, and the line of the clan is merely a collection (*ensemble*) of rebirths and deaths of individuals who are always the same. (II: 138)

This passage contains most of the elements of the *personnage*, though it does not explicitly mention rituals, dancing, masks, myth or the way in which names typically skip one or three generations. Many references to the subject appear about this time. For instance from 1910 one might note the treatment of alternating generations among

Pacific coast tribes (III: 81) and the review dealing with West Africa (II: 180, with its reference to Vergil's phrase 'Tu Marcellus eris' [*Aeneid* 6.883]). Later, in 1925, when reviewing Trobriand and Ashanti materials (III: 131–33), Mauss refers to the complex of ideas as more widespread than had been apparent.

The idea of a sociological approach to the categories of the philosophers has an equally long history. It is foreshadowed in 1903 (II: 88), and several of the categories, though not the person, are treated together as such in 1908 (I: 28ff., which builds on 04, *SA*: 111–12). The locus classicus is no doubt Durkheim's treatment of the theory of knowledge in 1912 in *EF* (12–26; 627ff.), but although this work discusses the category of the 'personnalité' with reference to Australian ideas of the soul, it fails to follow up Mauss's central observation about the finite stock of names and souls.

As for the later transformations of the *personnage*, a few hints appear in early book reviews. In 1905 Mauss noted an interesting treatment of the contrast between the egalitarian individualism characteristic of Christianity and the aristocratic outlook of the Greek philosophers (II: 647), while in 1907 he touches on the significance of Jewish sects around the time of Jesus in the development of ideas about the individual and his *conscience* (II: 589). In 1920 (III: 616–18) he talks more generally of the proselytising religions as evolving and spreading the notion of humanity as everywhere identical; this was the context in which 'the notion of the individual disengaged itself from the social matrix and man gained awareness of himself'. In 1921, building on Fauconnet, he spoke briefly of the development of the notion of liberty, referring to the history of Roman law, to Christian notions of original sin, to 'the appearance of the individual *conscience* of the metaphysical person' and to the Latin *persona* (II: 123). In 1929, stimulated by Lévy-Bruhl's insufficient account (already mentioned) of the tribal name-soul connection, he finally related the *persona* to his prewar work on the 'personnalité' (II 132–5). Another stimulus may have been the Indologist Hopkins, whose account of the notions of the soul and self had interested him in 1925 (I: 161). Certainly in 1930 he was planning to deal with the topic in a festschrift for the Japanese historian Anesaki (1979: 216).

Thus the central themes of *The Person*, and indeed his attitudes towards evolution and philosophy, had been part of Mauss's thinking for more than three decades. Similarly, many of the less prominent themes can be followed up elsewhere in his work. The brief reference to linguistics relates to his 'Whorfian' interests, to his view of language as giving access to a range of categories additional to those recognised by philosophers. He was particularly influenced by Meillet's study of male/female and animate/inanimate in the gender system of

Indo-European languages (37, III: 551; cf. 39, II: 166), and he had nourished great hopes for the work on Bantu noun classes of his student Bianconi, who died in the Great War (25 III: 491–92, cf. 07, II: 97–99). When he referred to 'great' and 'small' as categories (24, *SA*: 309), it was apparently with reference to North-West Amerindian languages (1964: 126), or perhaps to Maasai (06, II: 543). Linguistic categories might of course be related to sociological ones: he once thought that he could glimpse a way of relating Marcel Cohen's work on Semitic tenses to Hubert's on time (27, III: 192). In *The Person* the footnote reference to the technical use of 'person' in grammar, and the problem of deixis alluded to in Mauss's Introduction, are both intriguing (see Benveniste 1966). I suspect, from his reference to writing 'the history of abstraction and categorisation in human cognition' ('dans l'esprit', 1948: 28), that he had in mind an evolutionary trend towards greater grammatical independence of the speaker from the subject matter of his statement. This would in a general way be parallel to the increasing separation (theoretically) of the legal person from his position in society. Perhaps there would also be a parallel to the relationship of perceiver and perceived: 'until the sixteenth century, following Plato, it was believed that, if man could see, it was because his eye possessed the ability to project a luminous ray onto the things he saw' (*M*: 205).

In the paragraph specifically on psychology the Introduction distinguishes sharply between a pan-human sense of the self – a biological given, present in everyone – and the variable concepts created around it by each society. However, by the end of the essay the sociological notion of the person is well on the way towards identification with the psychological, and the relationship between the two could be explored at any point in their history. Mauss was particularly interested in the fact that under certain circumstances a healthy member of a tribe may die within days without any apparent illness: 'his vital energy is broken because he has been separated from the psychological support constituted by the religious society of which he is part' (23, III: 282). The phenomenon interested him both for its relevance to Durkeim's work on suicide, and as bringing the social, psychological and biological into the most intimate contact (26, *SA*: 329–30).[6] It is relevant, too, to note that among primitives moral systems tended not to be interiorised as a *conscience* (*M*: 200), and that in the evolution of prayer and other religious phenomena the two great currents were spiritualisation (i.e., interiorisation) and individualisation (09, I: 361). Native theories of individual artistic creation might also be cited. In ancient Greece the work was extracted from the poet by his Muse, while often elsewhere it is revealed to him by spirits (*M*: 235); the active agent is external like the soul reincarnated in the tribal.

Arts, crafts, aesthetics

The above brings us back to the Kwakiutl masquerade, with its components of theatre, ballet and ecstasy. Apart from his personal interest in the arts (Cazeneuve 1968b: 9), Mauss attached great academic importance to aesthetic phenomena, for example, in the *Manuel*, thinking that, together with demography and human geography, linguistics and material culture, the subject had been unduly neglected by the prewar *Année* (27 III: 190ff.). One might distinguish three aspects to the importance of the arts. The psychobiological effects of collective rhythmic movement and vocalisation attracted his attention early on (03, II: 251; 393), for they helped to explain belief in the effectiveness of prayer and oral ritual (04, I: 548; 21, II: 122). They were the sort of phenomenon that needed to be included in the study of the whole man (24, *SA*: 305), for human sociology was only a component of anthropology, that is, human biology (34, III: 313). Secondly, the ethnographer should be particularly sensitive to the *mixture* of the arts (*M*: 87), to the way in which dance may be associated with drama, singing, chanting, music, the decoration of the body or of objects, even with that proto-architecture recognisable in the preparation of a clearing for an Australian initiation (*M*: 107, cf. *EF*: 533). Above all, Mauss was fascinated by the context in which all these activities typically take place, i.e., the *fête* or ritual gathering, which represented for him the acme both of the sacred and the social.

Consider his well-known contrast between the secular, dispersed lifestyle of the Eskimos in summer, and the concentrated communal life of the winter settlement. The latter is passed, 'one could almost say, in a state of continuous religious exaltation ... a sort of prolonged *fête*'. Social life is marked with a sort of holiness and is collective in the highest degree. The heightened sense of the oneness of the community sometimes embraces the ancestors, of all generations since mythical times, who are summoned to become incarnate in their living namesakes and to take part in the exchange of gifts (06, *SA*: 444–47). It was this concept of the *fête* that enabled him (with Hubert) to write of 'the identity of the sacred and the social' ('est conçu comme sacré tout ce qui, pour le groupe et ses membres, qualifie la société', 08, I: 16–17).

Of all *fêtes* the type that interested him most was the North-West Amerindian potlatch with its competitive gift exchange and its numerous functions: 'such a syncretism of social phenomena is, in our opinion, unique in the history of human societies' (10, III: 33). This interest led to his best-known essay, *The Gift*, and its best-known phrase 'the total social fact' (25, *SA*: 147; 204; 274). By this he meant phenomena which 'assemble all the men of a society and even the things of the society from all points of view and for always' (34, III: 329). The conception of society as humans plus things was standard in the Durkheimian tradition; the 'points of view' correspond to the various aspects of the occasion – religious, economic, legal, aesthetic, sportive, and so forth; and the 'for always' must be a reference to the presence of the ancestors, who will also be reincarnated in descendants. There have been some highly abstract discussions of the total social fact (see Cazeneuve 1968a: Chapter 8), but Mauss's concept was in fact characteristically concrete.

At the heart of the *fête* was the dance.[7] 'Dance is at the origin of all the arts', and it would be a good starting point for the study of games, with all their psychophysiological importance (*M*: 95; 91). Under the hypnotic rhythm of the tribal dance individuals merge, as it were, in mind and body, moving in unity like the spokes of a wheel. It was this sort of context that gave rise to the notion of *mana*, which underlies religion as much as magic (04, *SA*: 125–30).[8] Thus Preuss was largely right in seeing the origin of religion in dance and mimetic ritual (06, II: 243). The centrality of dance in tribal cultures clarifies the reference in *The Person* to the Kwakiutl and Arunta institutions of compulsory retirement for those too old to participate. More precisely, as Granet had shown for China, dancing was a test or proof of continued possession by the ancestral spirit (31, III: 16).

Apart from the masks themselves, material artifacts are given more space than one might expect in a crowded essay on 'la pensée humaine'. The Kwakiutl boat is used to emphasise the possibility of a macro-historical perspective on tribal cultures, but like the 'almost anecdotal' reference to the Haida pipe, it may have a more general purpose. The essay is explicitly a sample of the work of the French school of sociology, and the postwar Mauss attacked 'the fundamental error of mentalist sociology' (Lévy-Bruhl again? *M*: 203), and emphatically denied that his own approach derived all important ideas from social structure, religion and symbolism. For concepts of number and space, for the origins of geometry, arithmetic and mechanics, one should look to the crafts, to weaving, sailing, the potter's wheel, and the like (27, III: 185), even if the phenomena are often coloured by religious and moral values (34, III: 330). In a sense, Mauss saw human thought as operating by a sort of bricolage, although he did not actually use the metaphor Lévi-Strauss was to popularise. As an evolutionist he saw the process as cumulative, and to refer to it he favoured Meyerson's word 'cheminer', 'to make one's way' (34, II: 149). Thus the early Indian thinkers took the elements of their 'science' from anywhere and everywhere: the notion of universal substance was related to a throw in a game of dice, and 'does not our own philosophy still subsist on words borrowed from all sorts of vocabularies?' (11, II: 600).

'Humanity has built up its mental world by all sorts of means: technical and non-technical, mystical and non-mystical, using its mind
(senses, affect, reason) and its body' (24, *SA*: 309). These broad formulations stand forcefully near the end of their respective pieces.

Uncle and nephew

The continuity of Mauss's thinking is so striking that Leacock (1954:
69–70), noting the parallels in argument and ethnographic sources
between *PC* in 1903 and *The Person* in 1938, went so far as to conclude
that the 'real significance' of the latter lay in its illustration of Mauss's
evolutionist conservatism. Mauss himself, however, was well aware of
changes in his views. The study written with his uncle concerned the
tribals' systematic intellectual constructions of the cosmos, such as
constituted the first step towards scientific philosophies of nature (not
their ability to classify in everyday contexts [03, II: 82]). The argument
was that the classifications were originally modelled on the structure of
society: 'the world-view [*mentalité*] of the lower tribes directly reflects
their anatomical constitution' (06, *SA*: 4–5, cf. 08, I: 29). He never
expressed doubt about the general direction of the argument,[9] but in
1907 (II 95) he recognised that by neglecting subtotems it had given
too simple a picture of tribal structures. Among the Hopi the contents
of the natural world were parcelled out not only among clans but also
among their members, who bore the names of subtotems and were
associated with religious roles and hereditary masks; and Mauss relates
this to his earlier observations on tribes with finite stocks of names
(though one page reference is wrong, as so often). Similarly, in 1913 (II:
135), he talks of 'the hierarchy of classifications' among the Omaha
descending from totem to subtotem to individual.

In several instances (e.g., 27, III: 221, *M*: 161), this line of thought
led Mauss to develop or recast the views of his uncle who, following
Morgan, had exaggerated the amorphousness of the clan.[10] It was
necessary to make more explicit the various cross-cutting differentiating factors such as sex, age, generation, and locality (31, III: 13). Even
in systems of non-competitive total prestations, individual exchange
partners are precisely determined according to their place in society
(26, III: 109n). There is always individualism as well as communism in
a society – the problem is to determine their proportions, 'leur dosage'
(*M*: 126). Durkheim's concept of the 'mechanical solidarity' of juxtaposed segments, valuable in its time, was too simple to express the
nature of tribal social cohesion, just as, conversely, there was an element of amorphousness in modern egalitarianism (34, III: 319; see
Chapter 3 below).

Just as tribal social structure was more sophisticated than he had first realised, so was tribal cognition. Lévy-Bruhl, ignoring Durkheim's criticism in 1913, had persisted in overemphasising confusions and participations in primitive thought at the expense of contrasts, oppositions and differentiations (23, II: 126; 24, *SA*: 302; cf. already 04, *SA*: 71). Admittedly (37, II: 159), Durkheim, Hubert and he himself had formerly erred in the same way – perhaps Mauss regretted expressions like 'the complete lack of differentiation between sign and object, home and person, places and inhabitants' (01, II: 16). The so-called 'participations' were not mere confusions, but perfectly deliberate efforts to establish a connection or likeness (Greek *homoiōsis* 23, II: 130). Indeed Mauss in general put more emphasis than Durkheim on the *active* role of humanity in social phenomena.[11]

Homogenisation and the categories

By means of their identification with different *personnages* individuals indistinguishable in life-style are rendered qualitatively heterogeneous. This is the exact opposite of the modern egalitarian position that, however obvious the differences in power and wealth, all men are, in principle, equal in the eyes of the law, and one man's vote is as good as another's. In practice, personhood rarely has this sort of homogeneity beyond the borders of the nation state, and in 1920 Mauss held that, whatever the ultimate truth of the idea of man as 'citizen of the world', it remained utopian and without foundation in real interests or contemporary realities (III: 629); he thought national differences in intellectual culture were actually increasing (ibid.: 594). However, I think that he would have recognised over the next sixty years a further homogenisation of personhood, for instance in sex-equality legislation and in international attitudes towards human rights.

In evolutionary perspective (though Mauss never made the point as such) the same ironing out had affected the other categories. For many peoples space is profoundly differentiated, each region having its own affective value and *sui generis* virtues, whereas for us it is 'made up of parts which resemble each other and are mutually substitutable' (03, II: 86). The bloodless classes and taxa of the logician and natural scientist have developed from social groupings that were the object of differential sentiments deriving from religion and kinship (ibid.: 88 – western society does in fact contrast with most tribal ones in its prescription of more or less homogeneous affection towards all relatives). The scientific view of time as a uniform succession of instants and durations derives from religious calendars in which *fêtes* split up the continuum into periods regarded as qualitatively distinct (07, I: 50, summarising Hubert). Numbers, far from constituting a straightforward monotonic series, would in early culture have had rich and varied symbolic values – Mauss might well have thought of Granet (1934: Chapter 3), for they were intimate friends. As regards substance, the abstruse paper mentioned in *The Person* discusses a decasyllabic Vedic metre which was regarded as food for the gods (11, II: 595). Mauss's study was to have focussed on concepts of matter and food, and one might wonder whether the heterogeneity of the *personnages* would once have been conceived in terms of differing bodily substances deriving from differing totemic dietary rules – the tribal initiand is often given the power to eat the sacred animal (39, II: 164 – see now Allen 1998e). Totality, the category *par excellence*, had been treated in *EF* (629–35), a passage that Mauss thought unduly neglected (27, III: 185) and probably accepted (34, II: 150), and that developed ideas in *PC* (03, II: 84). The category was in origin the abstract form of the concept of society, and was probably closely related to that of divinity, but with the development of the wider horizons of world religions and internationalism it was becoming ever vaster, more purely cognitive, and more detached from its origins. The world no longer consists of tribes each with its own cosmos, and their dissolution is also a homogenisation, even if logically not of identical type to the process that has affected the previous categories.

As for cause, *mana* was the attribute, simultaneously material and spiritual (for the distinction was not sharp until Spinoza), of what exerts mystical power (*M*: 208; 245; a chapter revised in 1937–38).[12] Perhaps in this case Mauss would have argued that the essential evolutionary trend was a reduction of mystical causation to non-mystical, which would be another sort of homogenisation again. Moreover, a comparable reduction seems to apply in the other cases. Despite the deliberate effort of ritual, and the subjective reality that it creates (34, II: 151), and even if (as I would argue) early kinship systems in certain perfectly objective senses approximated the individual to a grandparent, the modern person is closer than the *personnage* to that which is actually the case. Mauss himself inclined to the view of Hegel and Hamelin that the truest and most fundamental categories appeared late in human history (21, II: 124).

Although *The Person* begins with the Aristotelian categories this was only the provisional strategy of the French school. Aristotle had been wrong to think that his logical analysis of the Greek language could by itself constitute the analysis of a universal mode of understanding (*logique*): there were other concepts and categories still to be discovered (*M*: 205), for instance those accessible through linguistics. Some were quite recent, for example, 'chance', as in 'games of chance'

(*M*: 94), or 'economics' – *homo economicus* really only dated from Man-deville (*M*: 125). We needed the largest possible catalogue of all the categories that mankind could be shown to have used. 'We shall then see that there have been, and still are, many moons, dead, pale or obscure, in the firmament of reason' (24, *SA*: 309, the well-known passage with which Lévi-Strauss ended his introduction to *SA*).

Concluding remarks

My purpose has been to understand *The Person* and the mind that pro-duced it rather than to assess the validity of its case. Could it be that, for all the long years of learning that lie behind it, Mauss's *personnage* is really a mirage? It would be a long job to re-examine the evidence on the tribal societies that Mauss mentions,[13] let alone to extend the analysis to others. My own experience and knowledge relate particu-larly to tribals belonging linguistically to the proto-Sino-Tibetan stock mentioned in *The Person,* but these societies are not very helpful. As one might expect, many isolated elements of the *personnage* complex are to be found, the totemic clans of the Kachari (13, I: 594), Tibetan masks (widely diffused, *M*: 101), the reincarnate dancers of ancient China (Granet), and so on, but not (to my knowledge) the finite stock of souls, names, and roles. Mauss would not have been disconcerted – clearly the great majority of societies lie between the poles he consid-ers, or off to the sides. If the hypothesis could be convincingly estab-lished for sufficient other areas, there would be nothing to prevent one supposing that in this region, too, sometime in prehistory, the domi-nant ideology was built around the *personnage*.[14]

   On a more theoretical note, the grand evolutionary perspective has largely been left in the background of social anthropology since Mauss's day, and indeed there is much to be said for a degree of humil-ity in the face of the general course of human history, 'a subject so vague and vast that no social anthropologist would be prepared to think it even meaningful today' (Lienhardt 1964: 10). However, acad-emic fashions change; archaeology, Marxism, sociobiology and the work on lexical universals are difficult to ignore entirely, and this aspect of Mauss's approach no longer seems particularly dated. If soci-ological world history is to be written by anyone, there can have been very few better equipped with the relevant knowledge than was he, and there is a vast amount to be explored in connection with the framework he suggested. For instance, at the start of his scale, the inheritance of the *personnage* from grandparents is no mere empirical curiosity: it would be the natural concomitant of the simplest logical possibility for kinship systems of the type most characteristic of tribal society, especially Australia, as I have suggested in a preliminary paper which owes much to Mauss (Allen 1982; cf. Chapters 3–4 below).[15]

Those distrustful of even Mauss's careful evolutionism can of course translate much of what he says into synchronic terms. One of the messages of *The Person* would be that, if one is interested in value systems, the *personnage* in the masquerade is more similar to the voter in the booth or the client in the Citizens Advice Bureau than to the film or television actor on the screen. Even so, however one reads the essay, if one reads it closely, it must be – for its length – as rich and as 'total' a piece of anthropological writing as one could find.

Notes

1. The full title is 'A category of the human mind: the notion of person; the notion of self'.
2. Karady followed up his useful introduction to the *Œuvres* with studies of the *Année* school as a sociological phenomenon in itself (1982; see also Besnard 1979). The 1973 Paris colloquium (*La notion de personne en Afrique noire*) is of more interest to Africanists than to Maussians, though one might contrast Fortes's reading of *The Person* with the present one. Like most commentators, Diaz (1979) concentrates on the major texts taken one by one. Several commentators seem to me overinfluenced by Lévi-Strauss's interesting but highly personal introduction to *SA*. Since *PC* was coauthored with Durkheim, the secondary literature on it is considerable. One might note Lukes (1973: Chapter 22) for valuable distinctions, Aston (1978: Chapter 3) for an interesting treatment of the essay qua text, and Bloor (1982).
3. The reason for starting with the Zuñi is in fact stated in the first sentence of the section devoted to them: 'Let us start with the phenomenon from which all these researches set off'. He means all the research on the categories, and is referring to the genesis of *PC*.
4. 'Just like the facts of religion, aesthetics, etc., juridical facts are enveloped in a diffuse formless mass, akin to law (*droit*), but without belonging to law properly speaking. Around religion, there is magic, divination and above all popular superstitions; around law there is *la morale*' (*M*: 199).
5. To a South Asianist, these seventeenth and eighteenth-century movements (whose importance in the development of political and philosophical thought 'can scarcely be exaggerated') recall the Indian sectarian movements whose significance as sources of innovation in Indian history has been so well emphasised by Dumont (see note 15).
6. Such a 'total' phenomenon seemed to him incompatible with the dissociated and divided mentality of literate elites (24, *SA*: 306); in spite of progress in recent centuries (22, II: 483), the mentality of non-elite Europeans, especially women, remained more unitary. However, by the 1930s at any rate, he was stressing the lack of an adequate sociology of women, or of women in relation to men (31, III: 15; 34 III: 341; *M*: 214).
7. Mauss's nearest approach to a field trip (ignoring his meeting with some Hopi in Washington, *SA*: 38, *M*: 204) was a three-week visit to Morocco, during which his personal objective was to learn about a certain cultic dance (30, II: 565–66).
8. In exploring Hubert's contribution to *EF*, Isambert (1976: 38) comments on Durkheim's rather sparse acknowledgement of the work of his disciples, and I think

this applies particularly to Mauss. Mauss used 'Elementary Forms of Religious Life' as a title both in his Inaugural (02, I: 90) and in the *Année* volumes 5–6, and Durkheim's treatment of the relationship between demographic aggregation and religious emotion is close to his own. Certainly after Durkheim's death Mauss made it clear that his own treatment of *mana* would have been more nuanced (23, II: 129), and he also had his own views on the belief in the soul: in the 1929 preliminary version of *The Person*, the cause of the belief is in part the necessity to name the individual and specify his social position among the dead and the living (II: 125). This is considerably more precise than Durkheim's view of the soul as 'the totemic principle incarnated in each individual', or his derivation of 'the notion of person' from an impersonal spiritual principle associated with the group, taken together with the bodily discreteness of the group's members (*EF* 355–56; 386). By 1933 (II: 143) Mauss felt that Hertz (following Robertson Smith) had overemphasised dualism, and that the early *Année* in general had in this respect oversimplified the notion of the sacred. Mauss might also have given less weight to emblems (*M*: 245).

9. The argument would have been clearer if they had distinguished more directly between two possible interpretations of the hypothetical link between society and cosmology: as an evolutionary *event* whereby systematic cosmologies originally came into existence, and as a matter of *covariation* thereafter, at least in the simpler societies. Mauss (who provided all the ethnographic materials for the essay, 1979: 210) probably supported both interpretations. For his role in converting Durkheim to the use of the ethnographic materials rather than literature on the ancient world, see Condominas (1972: 130).

10. His self-sacrificing work on behalf of deceased *Année* associates has often been remarked on, but this loyalty did not preclude constructive criticism. The reminiscences of those who knew him, such as Waldberg (1970), show an attractive personality, far from austere, in spite of the formidable learning. Clark (1973: 182) transmits the anecdote of Mauss, then around forty, hiding behind an orange tree in a café to avoid being seen by Durkheim when he should have been at work. In his own writing the warmth of character is most apparent in the obituaries, especially perhaps those of Sylvain Lévi (35, III: 535) and Alice Hertz (1928). For his political attitudes see (as well as the conclusion to *The Gift*) the article on Bolshevism (1924: 116): 'At the risk of appearing old-fashioned and a trotter-out of commonplaces we come back plainly to the old Greek and Latin concepts . . . of that necessary "friendship", of that "community" which are the delicate essence of the City'. One is reminded of the 'delicate and precious' idea of the person, that Idea that could disappear with us.

11. Already in 1901 (III: 148ff.) Mauss saw problems in using Durkheim's 'constraint' as a criterion of the social, preferring to define it as 'all the ways of acting and thinking which the individual finds preestablished and whose transmission takes place generally via education'. He particularly emphasised the notion of expectation (*attente*) with its psychological and quantifiable connotations (04, *SA*: 123; 23, *SA*: 306; 34, II: 117–18).

12. For Mauss, the prototypical example of *mana* was perhaps a tribal dance exerting its magical action at a distance. His vivid image of the Dayak women dancing with their sabres constrasts markedly with the extreme abstraction and intellectualism of Lévi-Strauss's treatment of the same topic (*SA* xlvi ff.). This is characteristic: The *Person* presents, not a composite generalised portrait of the personnage, but precise facts on specific societies, even quite long quotations from the ethnographers. We have repeatedly noted his interest in the concrete, the material, the biological. Another side to this realism is his attitude to statistics: he had always had 'an

intense certainty, almost a physical awareness, that there is nothing in society except statistical totals' (21, II: 125), and as a student he had considered specialising in quantitative studies (1979: 214). He often uses the verb *doser* 'to estimate the relative proportions of one thing in another'.

13. Cazeneuve (1958), returning from fieldwork with the Zuñi, argued that the data from that society did not in fact support the argument of PC.

14. In defining the theme of *The Person* I emphasise words such as 'public' and 'ideology' because a society's values are not necessarily unitary, and in any case 'that fragment of our life which is our life in society' is not all that needs studying (26, *SA*: 329). Mauss would have been the last to deny a universal psychobiological component, a sense of common humanity, in moral attitudes to the individual. If a toddler has hurt himself and needs comforting, what would it matter who is or is not a *personnage?*

15. Another interesting task would be to relate the work of Mauss to that of his pupil and continuator Dumont (esp. 1983). Dumont remarks (1979: xxix), in criticism of some American work: 'I do not think that the comparison of societies should be carried out under the rubric of their conception of the human person, since the latter is in my view something which is fundamental for some societies but not for others, even if every conception of society necessarily implies a certain manner of conceiving men'. Mauss would not necessarily have disagreed, since his essay was concerned not with the comparison of whole ideologies but with the development lying behind the modern form of the conception. One welcomes any attempt to update Mauss's philosophical vocabulary, but the problem of identifying cultural universals exactly, and of deciding whether or not they are *a priori* necessary, will no doubt be with us for a long time.

Chapter 2

PRIMITIVE CLASSIFICATION: THE ARGUMENT AND ITS VALIDITY

Among the works of Durkheim and his close collaborators, *Primitive Classification* (hereafter *PC*; I deliberately use the English title rather than the French) is one of those that Anglophone social anthropologists are most likely to read and even to own. But what do they make of it? Some of the students to whom I set the text find it almost entirely baffling, and few will find it easy reading. Now that it is so common for anthropologists to incorporate autobiography into their ethnography, perhaps I can do the same with a topic that belongs to anthropological theory and intellectual history.

It is October 1965, the second tutorial for a complete beginner in the subject. My supervisor, Rodney Needham, has published his translation of Durkheim and Mauss (1903) two years previously (when he was about forty). He assigns it for my weekly essay and encourages me to buy it. Nearly a third of the book consists of his 42-page Introduction, which is in four parts (Needham 1963). Part I is about the need for a translation: classification is the prime and fundamental concern of social anthropology, and this pioneering essay on the subject has been neglected. Part II presents what the translator sees as the essence of the argument, together with its defects – logical, methodological and general. The judgement is severe: the Frenchmen's argument is logically fallacious, methodologically unsound and very possibly devoid of any validity whatever (ibid.: xxix); indeed, the entire venture is misconceived (ibid.: xxvi). Nevertheless, Part III proposes that the essay retains some value: historically, it has been influential; methodologically, there is something to be said for it; above all, theoretically, it draws attention to the notion of classification. The notion is a vague one, but if anything this seems to the translator a virtue. Part IV deals with translation, both generally, as a worthwhile activity for academic social anthropologists, and specifically, as regards the problems raised by this particular text.

The whole introduction is written with great verve, radiates self-confidence, and refers to an impressive and useful range of anthropological literature. No doubt at the time I assumed that it was authoritative. Perhaps I felt, as some students may do today, that after such an introduction, it would be a waste of time to do more than skim the text itself, densely packed as it was with confusing details about Australian Aborigines, Amerindians and Chinese. One already knew that the argument was all wrong, and that the central lesson to be drawn from the essay was that anthropology was about classification.[1]

Over the years, while remaining grateful for having been introduced to the work, I began to have doubts about the mode of introduction. In a general way, as students ought to, I came to recognise that no supervisor is likely to be right about everything. Fieldwork contributed to the recognition, since an unelaborated notion of classification, though it marked some of my early ethnographic papers (e.g., Allen 1972), seemed to carry me only a limited distance in understanding Hinduising Himalayan tribes. Moreover, my various more theoretical endeavours seemed in one way or another to suggest that Durkheim and Mauss might have been on the right track after all. I shall discuss three of these lines of work, the first two rather briefly.

Firstly, comparative work on Himalayan kinship and social structure led me to an abstract theory about kinship systems, which is explicitly world-historical in scope (Chapters 3 and 4 below). This has perhaps given me a greater-than-average sympathy for the evolutionist style of discourse that was normal when *PC* was being written.

Secondly, many reasons led me to develop a special interest in Mauss. Among these were the help he can give to kinship theorists (Allen 1989b: 53), and the acknowledged influence he exercised on Dumont, whose work on the Hindu world seemed destined to remain a landmark for a long time to come. Reading all of Mauss's collected works, I developed an immense respect for him, being particularly fascinated by his essay on the person. This led, via a lunchtime conversation with Michael Carrithers, to a paper (Chapter 1 above), published in a collection devoted to that essay. But Mauss's essay strongly resembles *PC*. So was the latter really as misconceived as its translator had claimed?

Thirdly, from the mid 1980s onwards, I tried to carry forward the work of Georges Dumézil. In the early 1920s Dumézil embarked on the study of comparative mythology under the influence of Frazer but, as he himself recognised, his work only 'took off' in the late 1930s after his contacts with Mauss and with the Sinologist Granet. So far as I know, he never cited *PC*. It was Granet above all whom he acknowledged, though he found it difficult to formulate the exact nature of his intellectual debt (1981: 21; 1987: 64; see di Donato 1983: 402–3). However, the matter is perhaps not entirely mysterious.

It was in 1934 that Dumézil started attending Granet's lectures, and it was in the same year that Granet published *La pensée chinoise*. The latter might almost be called *Chinese Primitive Classification*, so obvious and so explicit is the debt to *PC*: 'Chinese notions belong to a system of classification which it is entirely legitimate to compare with [*rapprocher de*] "primitive classifications"' (Granet 1934: 28). On the next page comes the oft-cited footnote 22 to the effect that *PC*'s few pages on China 'ought to mark a date in the history of Sinological studies'.[2] So we have two explicit connections: *PC* influences Granet, and very soon afterwards Granet influences Dumézil. It does not necessarily follow that *PC* lies behind Dumézil's significant work; but the evidence within that work is suggestive.[3] If so, anyone who aspires to build on Dumézil has reason to look at *PC* with a sympathetic eye.

If, however, from one point of view Dumézil is probably indebted to *PC*, from another he more than repays the debt. As I hope to show below, Dumézil's work gives considerable support to the argument of *PC*. Yet its own cogency lies internally, in the quality, quantity and interconnectedness of the analyses of Indo-European material, and is not dependent on its (hypothetical and indirect) source of inspiration. My argument therefore begins with Dumézil. Having looked to Saussure for theoretical assistance, I then turn to *PC*, especially to its ethnographic core, before returning to Needham. I have no space to react individually to the other commentators, in particular Lukes (1973: 446ff.), who in this context essentially follows Needham.

Dumézil and Saussure

Out of Dumézil's vast œuvre I am concerned only with his analyses of manifestations of the three 'functions' within the Indo-European speaking world. I shall have to be very curt, apologising to anyone who may be encountering this line of research for the first time. The results of trifunctional analyses can be usefully expressed in tables having the form of Figure 2.1: each row and each column has a label that expresses its unity, and each box in the matrix has at least one entry. The label for a row refers to the context or domain, from which the entries have been abstracted, while the label for a column is one of the three functions. A function is a cluster of ideas, whose unity was presumably 'felt' by the earliest Indo-European speakers (or their ancestors), and was recognised by Dumézil on the basis of his comparisons between different domains from different Indo-European

	F1	F2	F3
D1	*e*	*f*	*g*
D2	*k*	*l*	*m*
D3	*q*	*r*	*s*

Figure 2.1 Abstract form of Dumézilian trifunctional analyses.
Notes: F = function, D = domain

cultures. Sympathetic readers of Dumézil soon learn to recreate for themselves this sense of the identity and coherence of each function.

The rules for making entries in the table are quite strict. Within their original context (say, a certain ritual), the potential entries in a row must hang together and be homogeneous, distinct and exhaustive; simultaneously each entry must unambiguously fall under Dumézil's definition of the function associated with its column. In practice, Dumézil, being a comparativist, typically juxtaposes analyses drawn from different areas of the older Indo-European world, for instance a triad of gods from the Scandinavian pantheon with another triad from the Roman. But there is nothing to stop one assembling and tabulating all the analyses bearing on a single culture, say ancient Rome. Each row would now refer to a different domain within that culture. Thus, in Figure 2.1, *efg* might refer to a distinct segment of the king list, *klm* to the modes of marriage recognised in Roman law, *qrs* to the group of priests called *flamines maiores* (henceforth flamens). Other rows might be added to refer to yet further contexts or domains, perhaps to certain triads in the pseudo-historical narratives (such as the three tribes who originally came together to form the Roman people), or perhaps to a particular set of symbolic objects, or the alleged causes of a certain event. If one wishes, the individual rows can be grouped under headings such as pseudo-history, law, religion.

I believe that there are very many more rows yet to be identified in the Roman material (as indeed elsewhere), and also, more fundamentally, that we need to add two more columns (not necessarily filled in every row), one on either side of Dumézil's block of three (see Allen 1991). However, neither of these points is crucial to the comparison with *PC*, which turns on the abstract properties of the schema.

This brings me to Saussure and, more precisely, to his contrast (1985: 170ff.) between syntagmatic and associative (nowadays 'paradigmatic') relations.[4] These exist within a language (*langue*) regarded synchronically, and (at least in the words of his editors) correspond to two forms of our mental activity. Firstly, the meaningful units of language unroll over time, as it were along a line, and the relations that exist along this notional line of discourse are syntagmatic. They are relations *in praesentia*, because the units between that are related are effectively co-present (think of the components of a sentence). Secondly, any particular meaningful unit is associated with a whole constellation of other units with which it shares some feature or other. These associative or paradigmatic relations are *in absentia*, since they link a unit that has been selected for use with others that have not been selected. Saussure saw these latter relations as existing in the (normally unconscious) memory.

Dumézilian analyses are usually based on indigenous texts (only rarely on artefacts), and a typical context is thus a stretch of text. It may happen that the entries in a row of a Dumézilian schema appear as an uninterrupted sequence of words in the text, e.g., the triad of gods Jupiter, Mars and Quirinus. In such cases the relationships between units are obviously syntagmatic; but the situation would scarcely be different if the three gods were abstracted from a larger stretch of text, a myth perhaps, in which each of them played a comparable role.

Saussure, however, goes further (1985: 172). Syntagmatic relations hold not only between coordinate elements but also hierarchically, between the coordinate elements and the superordinate totalities that they form. *Contremaître*, 'overseer', is related syntagmatically to *contre* and *maître*, since the whole and its parts are equally copresent in the line of discourse, albeit on different analytical levels. The analogy in the Dumézilian case is between the individual entry (the part) and the label for the row (the whole), e.g., between a particular flamen and the three flamens regarded as a group.

So, are the relations between the entries in a column paradigmatic? Certainly they are, generally, *in absentia* – the stretches of text in which we encounter the F1 original tribe are different from those in which we encounter the F1 mode of marriage, the F1 king, etc. But by the rules of the method, the entries in a column are necessarily related at least insofar as all pertain to the cluster of ideas that defines one function (though the relation may of course be closer than that). All the entries in the F2 column relate somehow to physical force or war. However, the idea that these relations exist in the subconscious memory of individuals is here problematic. Occasionally one row is linked to others in a way that is obvious: the relation between the three flamens – *dialis*, *martialis* and *quirinalis* – and the canonical triad of gods must have been no less obvious to the Romans than it is to us. But in general one simply does not know how much awareness there was of the 'vertical' associations recognised by the analyst, or how far such awareness could have been induced by judicious questioning. Very likely it was often non-existent by the time our evidence entered the written record, but present at some (unspecifiable) period in the more distant past.

In spite of this difference, two further points justify us in describing the vertical relations as paradigmatic. I quote Saussure (1985: 174): 'Whereas a syntagm immediately calls to mind the idea of an order of succession and a fixed number of elements, the terms in an associative [i.e., paradigmatic] family do not present themselves either in a definite number or in a fixed order'. This applies precisely to our case, and we shall find it useful later. Consider the number of entries in a Dumézilian row. They are not always three, for there may be more than one entry per box; but the number is always fixed (and, one might add, usually fairly small, very seldom reaching double figures). Secondly, it is characteristic of manifestations of the three functions (though not invariable) that the texts present them in the order of the functions. In contrast, the number of rows one could write for Roman culture is not fixed;[5] and the order in which they are presented is arbitrary, i.e., chosen by the analyst with a view to expository convenience or rhetorical effectiveness.

Regarding rows, we argued – following Saussure – that the relation between entries and label is syntagmatic, so what can we say regarding columns? The analogy between language and the Dumézilian schema is not immediately helpful here, since a particular linguistic unit is related paradigmatically not to a single set of units such as could be written in one column, but to multiple sets. Starting from *enseignement* ('teaching'), Saussure's diagram shows separate sets radiating in four directions and consisting, respectively, of other derivatives of the verb, of semantic neighbours such as *éducation*, of other words with the same suffixed morpheme, and of words that merely rhyme. Nevertheless, the relation between a function and its manifestations is one of likeness *in absentia*, and must be classed as paradigmatic.[6]

So far we have been looking at the Dumézilian schema synchronically, as a summary of aspects of early Roman culture. What can we say about it diachronically? Presumably, if we could trace it back in time, we should find both greater pervasiveness of the three- or four-functional organisation through the various domains of social life, i.e., more rows, and a clearer apprehension by the people themselves of the conceptual links between entries in a column. But this is only inference. What about the subsequent history, which we can document? In general, as the centuries pass, each domain becomes transformed in different ways. With the coming of Christianity, the old triad of gods with their flamens becomes obsolete, as does the old legal triad of modes of marriage. The narratives about ancient kings and about the original tribes of Rome become precisely 'ancient history', irrelevant to all but scholars, unknown to the wider public unless fragments of them appear in school textbooks or can be used by the tourist industry.

And the new institutions and narratives do not fit into the schema. For modern Italian culture a Dumézilian schema of anything like comparable scope is out of the question. The style of cognitive ordering embodied in the schema has simply dissolved.[7]

Primitive Classification

With these ideas in mind I turn to *PC*. I start not with the 20 percent of the essay that makes up the writers' Introduction and Conclusion, but with the remaining 80 percent. We shall see that much of what Durkheim and Mauss are saying can be summarised in schemata comparable to the Dumézilian one; and I hope to show that the analytical language we have been developing helps to clarify their argument.

Australia

The ethnographic core of *PC* has four parts. Part I starts with Australia, which the writers think offers the humblest classifications on record. Before coming to particular tribes, they generalise about aboriginal social structure. A typical tribe is divided into two moieties, each of which is subdivided in two cross-cutting ways: it is split into a certain number of clans, each associated with a totem, and it is also split into two marriage classes or 'sections'. We can here ignore the rules of marriage and recruitment that define these social units (see Chapter 3 below), but it is worth illustrating the two structures in branching diagrams (Figure 2.2).

Straightaway we have a classification: members of society are allocated unambiguously to moieties, clans and sections. What is more, we have, in our terms, a two-level hierarchical classification, moieties being superordinate to clans or sections. Now comes an important italicised phrase such as one regularly finds near the start of *Année sociologique* texts. The thesis which their Part I will try to demonstrate, and which has not been stated previously, is that the classification of things reproduces that of people (i.e., into the units of social

totality of tribe

moieties

sections (4); clans (7)

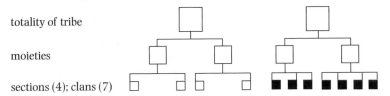

Figure 2.2 Stylised depiction of Australian social structures.

structure). The evidence comes mainly from four tribes:[8] two from Queensland, where the relevant social units are moieties and sections, and two from the South-East, where they are moieties and clans. Can we summarise the analyses in schemata comparable to Figure 2.1?

Units of social structure appear not uncommonly as rows in Dumézilian schemata; the obvious example is the list of *varṇa* categories so salient in accounts of traditional Hindu social order. In the Australian case, comparable lists of sociostructural units were presumably elicited by the ethnographers when they questioned their informants. The units in such lists could reasonably be described as hanging together and being homogeneous, distinct and exhaustive; and I suspect that, like the *varṇas*, they were often enumerated in a standard order. In any case, one can envisage a domain labelled 'society' and consisting of units related syntagmatically.

A problem that rarely arises in the Dumézilian case is how to show the multilevel nature of the sociostructural classification in a two-dimensional diagram. 'Levels' are normally shown vertically, as in Figure 2.2, but we shall need the vertical dimension of the page for paradigmatic relations. One solution is to envisage the branching diagram as lying in a third dimension, on a plane extending backwards behind the page. We need not actually try to draw this third dimension, but can distinguish superordinate groupings from their subordinate units by using thicker lines to separate the former. The highest level of the branching diagram identifies the context or domain, and appears at the left end of the row.

If it is true that the classification of things reproduces that of men, is the relation between a class of the one sort and a class of the other paradigmatic? The relation is *in absentia* since, in general, it is in the mind, rather than in a spatio-temporal context such as a list, that natural species and objects of various kinds are associated with units of social structure. Moreover, the species associated with a particular unit are often indefinite in number and come in no fixed order (unless one wants to say that the totem itself comes first).

When we draw the relevant diagrams (Figure 2.3), we need only two rows, one for the humans in their social units, the other for the rest of the contents of the cosmos. The aborigines could obviously have distinguished different domains within the cosmos, but the sources used by Durkheim and Mauss say little about this. Thus, as regards number of rows, the extreme simplicity of this first set of diagrams is misleading. For tribe 1, the labels L1 and L2 refer to the native terms Yungaroo and Wutaroo, which label simultaneously the moieties of society and the two halves of nature into which everything else is classified.[9] Tribe 2 is only slightly more complex. If the original ethnographic data and the interpretation are reliable, the two-level

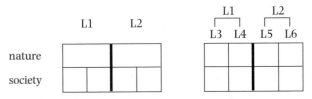

Figure 2.3 Queensland tribes.
Notes: On left, tribe 1 (Port Mackay); on right, tribe 2 (Wakelbura). L = label.

classification of society into moieties and then into sections applies also to nature. The authors emphasise the pervasive relevance of the classification to various cultural contexts – to dietary rules, ritual, divination and the use of message-sticks.

The South-Eastern tribes (Figure 2.4) classify nature according to their totemic clans. In both cases the clans are distributed into two named moieties, but it is only in tribe 4 that this is relevant to the classification of nature. In both cases the species or entity used as the totem provides a category label both for the other natural species in its column and for the members of its clan. Durkheim and Mauss here make an important distinction (II: 29, tr. 20). Whereas clear-cut discriminations exist between what (in our terms) are entries within rows, the demarcations encountered as one moves up and down the schema, i.e., between rows, are extremely permeable. As for the native conceptualisation of the vertical or paradigmatic relations, in some cases, as in tribe 1, the natural species or object (e.g., a crocodile or the sun) is just said to 'be' Yungaroo or to belong to that moiety; in other cases the relationships are conceived of in terms of kinship, closer or more distant, or in terms of 'flesh', friendship or property.

Part II of *PC* asks how widespread are such classifications in or near Australia. The ethnography cited here does not give rise to such clear-cut holistic schemata as in Part I, but is interpreted in terms of historical derivation from, or incomplete reflection of, such schemata. In Mabuiag (Torres Straits) we have moieties called respectively 'small' and 'great', and linked with certain other binary oppositions, as well as with totems and associated species or artefacts. The main difference from previous configurations would lie in the punctate or fragmentary nature of the rows, whose entries might perhaps better be shown

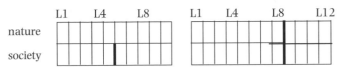

Figure 2.4 New South Wales tribes.
Notes: On left, tribe 3 (Mount Gambier); on right, tribe 4 (Wotjobaluk).

as blobs than as boxes. A systematic classification of the contents of
the cosmos gives way to what looks like the relics of one. Similarly,
Australian astral mythology is viewed as an expression within one
domain of present or earlier systematic classifications. Part II is interesting particularly for its emphasis on diachrony, on the transformations to which the classificatory schemata are liable. Thus the Arunta,
who have more than fifty-four totemic groups, prompt a discussion of
segmentation, i.e., of the splitting of social units, and of their *émiette-
ment*, their disintegration or crumbling into fragments.

North America

Part III, the longest, deals with the Zuñi of New Mexico and with some
Sioux groups, before returning to the Australian Wotjobaluk (our tribe
4). The Zuñi resemble the tribes of Part I in that their classification of
the universe is in principle exhaustive and systematic. Apparently, it
was Cushing's ethnography on this group that provided the initial
stimulus for the essay (Chapter 1, note 3 above). The account starts
with what we have been calling the column labels, which in this case
are the four cardinal points plus zenith, nadir and centre. They are
shown in Figure 2.5 in the 'natural' or 'normal' order of listing, i.e.,
anti-clockwise starting in the north. The sequence forms a descending
hierarchy, but in some contexts the centre can be 'first as well as last'
(Cushing 1896: 369–73). Under these headings the whole cosmos is
parcelled out – seasons, elements, animal species, social functions,
colours and (here we encounter the second recourse to an italicised
statement) the traditional set of nineteen matrilineal clans, organised
in six groups of three, with the central clan as a loner. A clan has direct

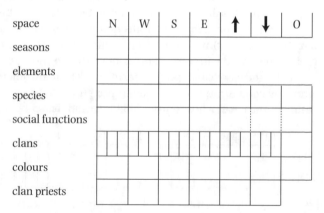

Figure 2.5 Zuñi (New Mexico).

paradigmatic links with a region of the *pueblo*, with a colour and a totemic species (from which it takes its name), and also, in a qualified sense, with a social function.

As for the history of the schema, Durkheim and Mauss suggest that the nineteen clans derive by segmentation from seven proto-clans. They see traces of an even earlier phase in a grouping of six priests associated with six of the clan totems, and perhaps in the six recognised classes of wild game that are linked with six of the regions – the last region to be added would have been the centre. Finally, they raise the possibility of an even earlier fourfold phase when the clans were arranged in two moieties, as suggested by a creation myth referring to two pairs of eggs.

The original title of the essay (abbreviated in the translation) is 'Of some primitive forms of classification'. The authors have now recognised two main forms or types (they use the terms interchangeably). In the Australian type the labels for columns are provided by totems or units of social structure, while in the Zuñi type they are provided by regions of space or, in another formulation, by oriented clans. Much of Part III is devoted to arguing, on evidence drawn first from the Zuñi and then from elsewhere, that the second type derives from the first, that the gap between them is bridged by intermediate forms. The Sioux, as it were, point backwards to the Australians, while the Australian tribe 4 is typologically closer to the Zuñi than are the Sioux.

Among the Sioux, the Omaha are treated at greatest length. Their highly segmented totemic patriclans are organised in moieties and associated with social functions and with a large number of species and entities. When the tribe sets up camp, the units of social structure have fixed positions relative to the line of march. Thus social units are related to space, but only to the space of the camp and only relative to the direction of movement – not absolutely to cardinal points. In contrast, the Wotjobaluk clans are related absolutely to fixed portions of the horizon, i.e., effectively to cardinal points, even though no link is reported between the cardinal points and categories of nature. Comparable linking of social structure and directions occurs in Mabuiag at the level of moieties (leeward/windward), and at Aranda tribal gatherings. Part III ends by modelling the transition from the Australian to the Zuñi type.

Non-tribal peoples

Part IV deals with the authors' third and last well defined form of primitive classification. In the first type, social structure itself virtually provided the column labels, and in the second it operated at one remove,

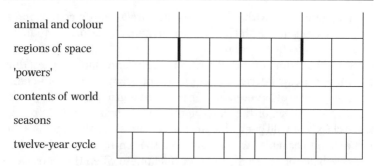

Figure 2.6 China (simplified).
Notes: An alternative schema mentioned in *PC* has five columns and three
    rows (elements, planets, regions of space).

via space; but in the third type, best exemplified by China, it is no
longer an integral part of the classification. The various more or less
conflicting schemata, which are of extreme complexity, embrace
nature, or much of nature, and various orders of time, but they do not
embrace society (Figure 2.6).

Having searched (unconvincingly) for direct evidence that the animals in the duodenary cycle were formerly totemic, the authors look
briefly at the similarities between Taoism and early Greek thought,
especially in the context of divination. Systems of divination depend
on classifications not unlike the tribal ones, and so do mythologies, for
example, those of the Indians or Greeks: well-organised pantheons
share out nature among their members, just as do totemic social
structures. The discussion of 'developed mythologies', which lie
behind the rise not only of monotheism but also of philosophy and
science, perhaps suggests a fourth type of classification, the mythological type, in which the columns would be headed by a hierarchically organised pantheon with henotheistic tendencies. In any case,
these allusions to the gods of Greece and India bring us back to the
Indo-European world of Dumézil. So let us now try and view the essay
as a whole.

Introduction and Conclusion

The Introduction proposes that the construction of logical and scientific classifications, with their clearly delimited taxa, is not an activity
naturally inherent in the individual human mind, but a social institution, which has developed over a long history. Even in the contemporary West, domains such as folklore and religion retain a prescientific
cognitive style.[10] In archaic literate cultures this style pervaded a

larger number of domains, while among the simpler tribes it was basic to conceptions both of mankind and of nature.

In the main body of the text the authors reverse the direction of their argument and start with tribes. The different types of organisation form an evolutionary sequence. In the simplest case, the units of social structure, the totems which represent them, and the associated components of nature all form a close-knit unity. In the second type, the link between social structure and the rest of the classification passes via the conceptualisation of space in terms of cardinal points. In the third type, social structure and the classification of nature have cut loose from each other. The third type leads on to the genesis of scientific classifications in Greece.

The Conclusion is too rich for easy summary, but the main point for us is the typological contrast between primitive and scientific classifications. Both types are hierarchically structured philosophies of nature,[11] but they differ in their relation to society. In the primitive type one should think of society as having originally provided not only the model or inspiration for the classification, but also its actual *cadres*, its framework and dividing lines. Moreover, the assimilations and differentiations that constitute any classification were originally based not so much on purely intellectual judgements of sameness or difference, as on the affective attitudes and evaluations that permeated social life. This was a major obstacle to the emergence of scientific classifications.

Criticisms

Among the translator's many criticisms of the essay, one concerns causation. The criticism is foreshadowed in his Part I, with reference to the prevailing neglect of *PC*: a certain publication devoted to the interdependence of social relations and cosmological ideas fails to mention the essay's attempt to demonstrate 'a constant causal connection between the two' (1963: x). The point recurs in his Part II as one of two general objections applying to the entire argument: 'There is no logical necessity to postulate a causal connexion between society and symbolic classification, and in the absence of factual indications to this effect there are no grounds for attempting to do so' (ibid.: xxiv).[12] The following page refers to 'the strength of [the authors'] preoccupation with cause', which leads them to present the facts as if society were the cause of the classification. They are 'explicitly concerned to propound a causal theory'.

But how much of this can be accepted?

1. The relation between social relations and cosmic classifications is not presented as constant, but as differing in the Australian, Zuñi, Chinese and modern cases.

2. Durkheim and Mauss do not explicitly characterise their theory as a causal one, and seldom use the vocabulary of cause and effect (not once in their Introduction). What they are most obviously propounding is an evolutionary theory – both the first and last paragraphs of *PC* use the word *genèse* (genesis) and the authors' central interest is surely in origins. Origins and causes are not unrelated, but the preoccupation with causes seems to be the translator's.

3. In so far as they do discuss cause and effect, one can distinguish claims relating to the long term and the short term. In the former case they talk of influences: they suggest that distant influences (spanning millennia) have left behind as an effect contemporary habits of mind that constitute the very framework of all classification (II: 88, tr. 88). But Needham's criticism relates to the short term. Here the authors use a variety of expressions: the classification of things is 'modelled on' social organisation, there is a close relationship (*rapport étroit*) between abstract ideas and the corresponding social organisation (ibid.). In the one passage where they do talk explicitly of causation, their causal arrow is not solely from society to classifications of things. When introducing the notion of segmentation, they propose that once a classification of nature has come into being, it can act back on (*réagir sur*) its cause (i.e., on the society which served as its model), and contribute to modifying it (II: 39, tr. 32).

4. In any case, whatever use is made of notions of causality, *PC* clearly presents social organisation as primary or prior to the classification of nature, as the prototype or basis on which the latter is modelled. Needham implies that there are no grounds for such an attribution of priority. Is this true?

To start with, Durkheim and Mauss are clearly not propounding a mechanistic synchronic law valid at all times and places. They know, as well as we do, or better, that the nineteen clans of the Zuñi have not generated nineteen regions of space, that the indefinite number of Chinese clans has not generated an indefinite number of columns in the Chinese schemata. They do not claim that the classification of things always reproduces that of men, or that the reproduction is so exact that moieties in society are inevitably accompanied by binary divisions of nature. The issue of a straightforward causal arrow only arises really clearly at the beginning of their evolutionary scale. It is here that we may try to choose between three possibilities. Were classifications of people extended so as to constitute classifications of nature (the Durkheim-Mauss view)? Or was society modelled on a classification of nature (the view which they attribute to Frazer and which Needham finds tempting)? Or should we simply envisage the set-up coming into being as a whole, and abstain from ascribing priority to either of its components (the view that Needham ultimately settles for)?

The topic is too large for full discussion here, but one line of argument can be sketched in support of *PC*. It is not unreasonable to argue that incest prohibitions mark the emergence of humans from prehumans. If one also accepts that such rules can be subsumed in the rules of marriage and recruitment that define social structures, then the latter are fundamental to humanity in ways that systematic classifications of the contents of nature are not: an early human society lacking a unified cosmology is a possibility, one lacking a social structure is not. Moreover, there are serious arguments for putting section systems similar to those of Australia near the start of a sociostructural evolutionary scale (see Allen 1989a: 182). In the absence of strong arguments in favour of the rival hypotheses, that of Durkheim and Mauss remains the best of the three.[13]

Needham's lack of interest in envisaging the genesis of classifications of nature goes together with an unsympathetic attitude towards the whole undertaking and, in particular, a tendency to gloss over the world-historical thrust of the argument. Thus, much weight is laid on the charge that Durkheim and Mauss repeatedly make unevidenced assertions. But insofar as it deals with archaeologically invisible aspects of non-literate societies, any evolutionary argument has to envisage changes that cannot historically be documented. The charge is not wrong, but it is not helpful. In this sort of discourse statements about change imply in the subtext a phrase such as 'In the light of our theory it looks as if . . .'.

Similarly the italicised statement at the start of Part I of *PC* is criticised (Needham 1963: xiv) as a *petitio principii*: to assert that the classification of things reproduces that of people is to assume what needs to be proved. No, it is simply to announce the hypothesis, in the light of which the evidence will be assembled and interpreted.

As for the fact that in many societies the correspondence between social structure and classification does not exist, or exists only partially, this was of course entirely obvious to Durkheim and Mauss. The lack of full correspondence is presupposed in their Part II, and stated emphatically in the opening to their Part IV. It is therefore pointless to demand that they test their thesis by demonstrating concomitant variation (ibid.: xvi), or that they pay special attention to negative instances. It is rather like asking Dumézil to devote a book to the absence of trifunctional patterns in the plays of Terence. What is interesting, and calls for explanation, is that some peoples do possess classifications embracing human beings and nature in a single simple schema; everyone knows that others do not.

The insensitivity to the world-historical aspect of the argument is illustrated by a reference to the Chinese case. This, says Needham, 'may be disregarded, since it exhibits no correspondence at all [sc. between society and classification], and its only value is that it shows that such classifications [sc. of nature] are not confined to simple societies' (ibid.: xxv). But its value for the argument of *Primitive Classification* is much more than this. Because of its richness and pervasiveness in social life, the Chinese type of classification serves to bridge the large gap that would otherwise exist in the sequence leading from the Zuñi type to the Greek and scientific types.

Needham's opening criticisms (ibid.: xii) concern Durkheim and Mauss's references to 'confusion' and lack of differentiation in the thinking of tribal people, and their suggestion that this sort of thinking survived in contemporary religious thought and folklore in the form of notions such as transubstantiation and metamorphosis. The phraseology of 1903 is clearly antiquated, indeed regrettable and misleading. No-one nowadays would say that a Bororo or an Australian 'confuses' a human with an animal. But the problem to which they were alluding has not disappeared, and we still lack a satisfactory analytical language in which to discuss it. In most societies, in some contexts, people do associate, or link, or identify elements from different domains in ways that scientists do not, and what is needed is not denunciation of 'gratuitous and implausible elaboration' (ibid.: xx), but an attempt to rephrase the problem in more appropriate language. It is here that the terms syntagmatic and paradigmatic may be helpful. Elements placed in the rows of our schemata and related syntagmatically are never confused with each other; on the contrary, their heterogeneity is more emphatic than in scientific classifications. The 'confusions' relate to elements placed in columns, i.e., to the paradigmatic relations.

Let us look more closely at two aspects of this issue. Durkheim and Mauss think that belief in transmutations could not arise if things were represented in the form of delimited and classified concepts (II: 15, tr. 5). Needham objects in effect (1963: xii) that to conceive of x being transmuted into y presupposes distinct concepts of x and y; thus the Frenchmen have committed a logical flaw. But these men were trained philosophers: were they really being so stupid or careless? Their point is that, to a modern and scientific mind, a human being and a parrot are classified in two quite separate domains, which are so sharply delimited from each other that the two entities cannot possibly be linked by physical continuity or transmutation. Other points of view or other societies no doubt see things differently: whereas a member of one clan is sharply delimited from a member of another, and a parrot is sharply delimited from a hornbill, in some contexts human and parrot, rather than being sharply delimited, 'participate' one in another (to use Lévy-Bruhl's term). It is as if the boundary between the concepts of human being and parrot were somehow fluid. The syntagmatic boundaries are unambiguous, the paradigmatic ones are not.

Secondly, under the heading of method and use of evidence, Needham (ibid.: xxii ff.) objects to the couple of pages on sentiment in the Conclusion of *PC*. He sees in them the abrupt and gratuitous introduction of a factor for which the previous text has provided no justification; and he finds it difficult not to recoil in dismay. However, this negative reaction neglects the discussion in Part I (II: 32, tr. 23f.) of how the Australians, or more precisely the Wotjobaluk, conceive of the relations between the groups composing their classifications. They do so, *tout d'abord*, in terms of closer and more distant kinship, so that the beings attributed to ego's moiety are his flesh and his friends, while his sentiments towards beings of the other moiety are quite different. More generally, one might comment that, if classification is related to social structure, the latter, especially in Australia, is interwoven with kinship, and kinship in turn is a matter of emotional links as well as genealogical ones. Thus, when in their Conclusion the authors raise the obvious question of how the contents of nature came to be allocated to the particular columns in which we find them, they have already prepared us for their answer, namely that the allocation involved sentiment as well as logic. The concepts of tribal peoples, they suggest, have strong affective connotations, positive or negative; the northern region of space is not merely an abstract direction, a compass point, but has qualities of its own, values or associations that will have a bearing on how it fits into the classification. These affective associations will contribute to the paradigmatic interdomain linkages, helping to maintain the permeability of the divides. Perhaps their idea raises more questions than it answers, but it is not obviously gratuitous. Would it be enough to seek purely cognitive explanations, and ignore affect?

Needham's most fundamental criticism, the one supposedly showing up the entire venture as misconceived, concerns Durkheim and Mauss's concept of mind. They subtitle their essay 'Contribution to the Study of Collective Representations' but, says Needham, when they talk about categories or about the classificatory function, their concern is really with the innate ability of the human individual, a topic belonging essentially to cognitive psychology. The charge is that their confusion on this issue invalidates the attempt to explore the origin of classifications.

No doubt Durkheim and Mauss could be clearer both in their concepts of mind (does not this apply to most of us?) and in their language, but the general orientation of the essay seems clear enough. It is indeed, primarily, about collective thought, about the prehistory of scientific classification, regarded as a social institution. They are not concerned with individual psychological capacities, but with the use to which these capacities are put in societies. Indeed, I suppose that, had they been questioned, they would have agreed that even animals possess the cognitive ability to make pragmatic classifications in the sense of 'rudimentary distinctions and groupings' (II: 17, tr. 7): a dog classifies some humans as friends, others as needing to be barked at or bitten. In any case, at no point do they even hint at any development in inborn cognitive capacities in the course of human history (incidentally they remark on the intelligence of one of Howitt's informants, II: 65, tr. 61). The essay is about philosophies of nature, and the issue of inborn capacities only arises because philosophers and psychologists suppose (wrongly) that such capacities are a sufficient explanation for the logical and scientific notion of a taxonomy.

PC is far from perfect. Although many of Needham's most emphatic criticisms turn out to lack substance, others are fully justified. Carelessness in the bibliographic citations and sheer misrendering of sources are of course to be deplored (1963: xlvi f.). Some of the speculations are indeed tendentious, or even totally unjustified, e.g., those about marriage rules in Siam. The authors do seem to contradict themselves on whether primitive classifications are primarily of practical or speculative significance (ibid.: xiii n. 3).[14] Moreover, the final paragraph contains a particularly unfortunate formulation, which may have been responsible for some of the misreading: 'We have already had occasion to indicate, in the course of the argument, how even ideas as abstract as those of time and space are at each moment of their history in close relationship with the corresponding social organisation'. No. They have tried to demonstrate this for a number of the tribal societies they have considered, but the statement does not apply to the literate ones. Three years later, at the end of his essay on the Esquimos, Mauss (*SA*: 475) was a little more precise, though his language has dated: *PC* had shown how the mentality [world-view] of lower tribes directly reflected their anatomical constitution [i.e., social organisation].

However, by far the greatest weakness of *PC* seems to me to relate to the 'technological classifications', treated so cursorily in footnote 225 (tr. 81 n. 1). What are they, and how do they fit into the argument? Possessed by mankind from earliest times, doing no more than express aspects of the praxis in which they are embedded, they are mere distinctions or divisions between ideas, not systematised, not constituting classificatory schemata (*tableaux*). Presumably they resemble the fragmentary distinctions and rudimentary groupings attributed to young children (II: 17, tr. 7). This suggests the following scheme:

evolutionarily ancient	A. primitive systematic philosophies of nature	B. technological classifications
modern	C. Scientific classifications	D. children's classifications (and unsystematised adult ones?)

The contents of B are left shadowy. The only concrete suggestion is a classification of components of the diet according to techniques of appropriation, e.g., of animal foodstuffs into fish, birds and land animals. But what about lower order taxa? Surely mankind always distinguished different species of land animal. However, this already implies a taxonomic hierarchy, which is supposed to be a feature of A, not B. No doubt, in 1900 very little was known about folk classifications of plant and animal species (ethnotaxonomies), but even at that time the question could have been raised. As we now know, such classifications may indeed be hierarchical, and they may have little to do with totemistic conceptions of the cosmos; moreover, they exhibit world-historical trends (e.g., Brown 1984, part of a significant body of work that might be called 'lexical evolutionism').

The obscurity surrounding B and its relation to A has important consequences. An initial disclaimer (II: 18, tr. 9) recognises that *PC* will not exhaust the question of how humans come to classify, and the opening of the essay (II: 13, tr. 3) emphasises that mental operations, faculties and functions may have a diversity of roots, being built up laboriously from the most heterogeneous components. Thus 'all sorts of foreign elements' may have entered into the development of the function they are concerned with (II 18, tr. 8). This foreshadowing of the notion of *bricolage* (characteristic of Mauss, as we saw in Chapter 1), may have been intended simply to prepare the reader for the heterogeneous contents of A (animals, cardinal points, etc.), since the authors are explicitly concentrating on the relationship A-C (footnote 225); but it seems to leave open the possibility of an input of B into C. In so far as B can be construed as embracing ethnotaxonomies, the authors would surely have been wise to leave this possibility open, as does, for example, Atran (1990), who is scarcely interested in A at all. To reduce the history of scientific classification to the history of the decline of the element of social affectivity (II: 88, tr. 88) is certainly to oversimplify.

Conclusion

So what is the value of the essay? It does much more, I think, than draw attention to a vague and indefinable notion of classification, worthwhile though that might be. In the first place, it establishes the notion of a primitive classification, which is a specific way of articulating a world-view, or at least considerable portions of that scarcely graspable totality. What characterises this particular type of classification (though the authors themselves do not use this terminology) is that it can be expressed in a schema made up of rows and columns, these alignments consisting of entities ('entries') linked respectively by syntagmatic and paradigmatic relations. By virtue of this property it contrasts radically with the type of world-view to which we are accustomed.

One way to envisage the relationship between the two is to imagine that, as the paradigmatic links between rows cease to be felt as 'real', the domains cease to be aligned vertically, and drift onto a single plane or line. It is not that, say, animals and metals cease to be related at all. They cease to be related paradigmatically, for the scientific world-view offers no support for vertical links; all that is left to the animals and metals is a remote symagmatic relationship resulting from their respective places within the animate and inanimate branches of a single hierarchical classification of nature. In this sense the world becomes 'flattened'.[15]

Secondly, the value of *PC* lies in the relation it posits between this type of world-view and social structure. It recognises three main phases in the relation. Originally, the social structure generates the classification of things. Subsequently, the predominance of social structure declines, and the two elements interact. Finally, the link is broken, and the primitive world-view itself declines, though survivals may linger in spheres such as religion, magic and folklore.

In trying to clarify the argument of *PC*, I have neglected relevant issues such as the relation of the essay to the intellectual milieu in which it was written, its place within the œuvres of its two authors, and its use of the anthropological material then available. But clarifying the argument is in any case only a first step towards the question of how far the authors were right. Here, my main point has been that a large body of relevant evidence is now available in the work of Dumézil and followers. The only reasonable explanation for these findings is that the speakers of proto-Indo-European, who were of course non-literate tribals, possessed a primitive classification. As for its origin, in spite of the cautious agnosticism of Dumézil's mature work (see Dubuisson 1991), the best explanation would seem to be that of Durkheim and Mauss. Typologically, in view of the correlations it makes between for example social functions, colours and types of priest, the Indo-European classification most closely resembles that of the Zuñi, and indeed one of the many consequences of recognising a fourth function is that it increases the resemblance, enabling one to include cardinal points and centre in the schemata for at least certain Indo-European cultures (see Allen 1991: 149; 1999b: 247–49). As for millennial trends in the Indo-European case, consider the increasing separation between social structure and the rest of the classification, and the lingering dissolution of the functional pattern in the latter. Are not such findings precisely the sort of thing that Durkheim and his nephew were predicting, over ninety years ago, in their astonishing essay?

Notes

1. The influence of this view lives on. See, for example, Chapman et al. (1989: 17), who talk of classification as 'an area of expertise that anthropology has made its own'.

2. By omitting 'ought to' (*devraient*), Needham (1963: xxii n.1), followed by Lukes (1973: 449 n.79) and Freedman (1975: 19), altered the force of Granet's remark.

3. I have cited elsewhere (Allen 1987: 38 n.2) the remark in Dumézil's 'breakthrough' article from 1938: 'It is rare, among the semi-civilised, that the classification of one category of concepts is not solidary with other classifications'. The use of the term *cadre* 'framework' in the three sources might also repay study – Durkheim and Mauss use it at least eighteen times. Might the lack of reference to PC be related to Dumézil's lack of enthusiasm for Durkheim, whom he regarded as too much a philosopher (1987: 48)?

4. A note on the history of ideas. Though influenced by Durkheim in some respects (Doroszewski 1933), Saussure here drew on the short-lived Polish linguist Kruszewski, who himself drew on British associationists (Jakobson 1971: 719). Dumézil (1987: 117) denies any direct influence from Saussure's *Cours*. For myself, I probably owe a debt to the papers of Edwin Ardener (see Ardener 1989, an important collection of essays), though my own use of the sytagmatic/paradigmatic contrast is narrower than his.

5. This is not only because further research is likely to result in new rows, but also because the number of rows one wishes to extract from a single context may be a matter of judgement.

6. In the final analysis it is the duality of the axes that matters, not the names one gives to them or to their labels. It is worth noting Saussure's discussion of the two factors involved in the notion of value (1985: 159ff.). A five-franc coin can be *compared* with like objects (e.g., a one-franc coin), and can be *exchanged* for unlike objects (e.g., a loaf of bread). One thinks of the differential social values attached to the functions or their manifestations and expressed in their numerical labels. Moreover, the one franc is subsumed in, and in that sense copresent with, the five francs, and Saussure envisaged the coin axis horizontally, the exchange axis vertically (Engler 1967:259 ff.).

7. Presumably this partly explains the incredulity with which so many scholars react to Dumézil's findings: the type of cognitive order he discovered lies outside their social experience.

8. I have omitted the evidence drawn from Palmer (1884), since it is neither well localised nor very clear.

9. Referring to the cosmology of tribe 1 in 1912 (*EF*: 201), Durkheim reports that natural objects are allotted not only to moieties but also, within them, to the clans. The same passage also alludes to tribes 3 and 4.

10. In discussing Durkheimian texts, one may be torn between trying to breathe new life into their dated phraseology, and trying to update it – thereby necessarily introducing anachronisms. The problem is of translating from 1900 to the present, no less than from French to English. 'Cognitive style' is not in the original, but I use it deliberately, hoping to imply the relevance of *Primitive classification* to more recent debates about, for instance, 'modes of thought' or 'rationalities'.

11. Cf. the phrase 'primitive philosophies' as used by Powell (1896: lvii).

12. Durkheim and Mauss do not talk of 'symbolic classification' or its French equivalent. They usually talk simply of the classification of things, or once (II: 15, tr. 5) of 'symbolic correspondences'. The English phrase was used as the title of a book by Needham which includes a summary of the earlier critique of *PC* (1979: 25–27).

13. Needham's initial preference for a reversed direction of causation is based on the argument that 'forms of classification and modes of symbolic thought display very many more similarities than do the societies in which they are found'. If this is so, as the China-Zuñi comparison might suggest, then within an evolutionary perspective it implies only that social structures tend to change faster than cosmologies.

14. However, the Introduction is not always accurate on details. Durkheim and Mauss do not claim regarding tribe 4 that 'a classification by clans preceded one by spatial regions' (1963: xx), nor do they refer to the prey animals as 'mediators between the Zuñi and their gods' (ibid.: xiii).

15. Perhaps the metaphor could cause confusion, since hierarchies are so often imaged by using the vertical dimension, as in Figure 2.2. However, in the imagery used in the other figures here, taxonomic hierarchies, with their relations of superordination and subordination, lie behind the page, at 90 degrees to it.

Chapter 3

THE DIVISION OF LABOUR AND THE NOTION OF PRIMITIVE SOCIETY: A MAUSSIAN APPROACH

It is easy for an anthropologist to criticise *The Division of Labour* (*DOL*). Like so much of Durkheim's thinking it is based on dualisms – primitive/modern, mechanical/organic, but the characterisation of the primitive pole has dated. The book was written before Durkheim had read much first-hand ethnography, when his conception of primitive society was based as much on the Bible and early European history as on contemporary descriptions of tribal peoples;[1] and even if read as an ideal type, his picture of primitive society now seems remote from realities. Homogeneous membership, near-perfect conformity to *conscience commune*, reliance on repressive penal sanctions – such features have often been criticised (Barnes 1966, Lukes 1973). Since most of us value disciplinary history, and since Durkheim's importance in anthropology is undoubted, his first book, which foreshadows most of the major themes of his *oeuvre*, must retain some historical interest; but one might doubt whether its view of primitive society has anything to contribute to the anthropology of the future.

My own view is more positive. In addition to its value for intellectual history, I argue that *DOL* poses questions that anthropology still needs to address, and gives pointers to the answers. My central question is, given that Durkheim's picture of primitive society is unacceptable as it stands, can it serve as a starting point from which to generate more satisfactory models?

I do not start from scratch. An anthropologist wondering what use to make of Durkheim still cannot do better than turn to Mauss. After his uncle's death Mauss consciously tried to develop Durkheim's theoretical ideas, and he did so in the light of his encyclopaedic knowledge of ethnography. Forty years after *DOL* was published, Mauss was still reacting to it, and my aim is to carry his reaction a little further. This approach has hardly been explored. There is no hint of it in the fifteen articles on *DOL* in Hamilton's anthology (1990 vol. II), nor in the sixteen contributions to Besnard et al. (1993).

Primitive solidarity

The term 'primitive' plunges us at once into anthropological attitudes to evolutionism – a complex issue, since this 'ism' can take such varied forms. The nub of the matter is the relation between tribal societies as described by ethnographers and palaeolithic societies as envisaged by archaeologists, between social/spatial remoteness from the metropolis and temporal remoteness from the present. It would be ridiculous to identify the two, as all would now agree. But it is equally ridiculous to rule out any relation at all, though such an attitude, at least in implicit or oblique forms, is common enough. Of course, one needs to discriminate. Ethnography from the globalised world of the 1990s will probably offer fewer pointers to earlier periods in the social history of our planet than the ethnography of Durkheim's and Mauss's contemporaries; and not all non-literate peoples are equally relevant. Mauss himself maintained that the tribal peoples on whom he mostly lectured during the 1920s and thirties were far less primitive than the Australian aboriginals on whom he had tried to write his thesis in 1909.

As to the word 'primitive' itself, we cannot nowadays use it with the unselfconsciousness of Durkheim or Mauss. The word is usually avoided because, in spite of increasing awareness of environmental issues (which may well make us ashamed of being modern), it is felt to be pejorative. But whatever terminology is chosen (primitive, small-scale, archaic, tribal, simple, technologically unsophisticated, etc), the question remains: can anthropology say anything at all about such societies, which would help us think about early human society? Many today would doubt it (cf. Kuper 1988), but I do not think we should give up the attempt. Other disciplines look to us for answers, and if we fail to supply them, they will invent their own.

As for 'solidarity', Durkheim does not give a formal definition in *DOL*, but Lukes (1973: 139) cites from an earlier paper his phrase 'the bonds which unite men one with another'. Durkheim also uses the term *cohésion*, which may carry fewer affective and subjective overtones. Whatever his reasons, this is the term that Mauss prefers.

Mauss regarded the topic of social cohesion as fundamental, and discussed it in various places. I draw mainly on three texts, from 1927, 1932 and 1934 respectively, which are collected in the third volume of his *œuvres*, but also on the lecture notes for his course on ethnography, the *Manuel*. The 1932 article ('Social cohesion in polysegmentary societies') seems to be the best known of these texts in the Anglophone world, though none has been published in translation.[2]

Mauss situated the topic within 'general sociology', a field covering those social phenomena that extend to the whole of social life (27, III: 227). The importance he attached to this field is clear from the *Manuel* (*M* 14), where his plan for the study of a society has three major headings: Social Morphology, Physiology (including technology, aesthetics, economics, etc.), and General Phenomena. He deliberately dealt with them in that order since the last-named express 'not only their own reality but also the solidarity of all the other phenomena among themselves' (34, III: 305). Unfortunately, in repeating his lecture course annually, Mauss never managed to cover the third heading before the end of the academic year.

When discussing social cohesion, Mauss was very aware of continuing his uncle's work: 'In a quarter century of writing Durkheim never lost sight of the problem of *l'ensemble* [the whole], which is basically that of the *DOL*, as it is of the *Elementary Forms*' (27, III: 183).[3] Or again: 'It is worth noting also that studies of this kind [directed towards a *sociologie générale*] were Durkheim's point of departure. For he considered his first great work, the *DOL*, not only as a fragment of moral physiology but also as a fragment of objective general sociology' (34, III: 303). However, Mauss was equally aware of the limitations of *DOL*:

> We all [Durkheim and disciples] set off with a somewhat romantic idea of the original form (*souche originaire*) of societies: the complete amorphousness of the horde, then [later in human history] of the clan; the communisms which flow from them. It has taken us perhaps several decades to free ourselves, I do not say from the whole idea, but from a significant part of these ideas' (32, III: 13).

Thus he holds that no society, however primitive, lacks a degree of differentiation, of *répartition des individus* (27, III: 221). In thinking that he could recognise the kindred horde in ethnography, Morgan, for all his genius, had simply been wrong, and as for Durkheim, his concept of amorphous societies at the origin of humanity was only a hypothesis – albeit, Mauss adds, a necessary one. Societies were divided by sex and generation, and very early on, by rules of exogamy. But as soon as one enters the realm of history or ethnography, and no doubt from well back in prehistory, one finds societies divided in another way too – into exogamous moieties, or more exactly, into two primary exogamous clans or phratries, and into clans within these phratries, and into families (27, III: 221–22).

How does this compare with Durkheim? When Durkheim introduces the notion of the horde as an absolutely homogeneous mass
lacking distinguishable components, totally without form or organisation, it is in an effort to imagine '*le type idéal* of a society whose cohesion is based solely on similarity' (*DOL* 149). Rather than Durkheim's
'ideal type' or Mauss's 'hypothesis', we can perhaps nowadays most
naturally call the horde a 'model'. Durkheim knew that ethnographers
had not described such a society (though he implied that they might
do so one day), and he saw the most primitive attested form of society
as being segmented by clans, and not on the basis of territory (*DOL*
161). Moreover, like Mauss, though at this period he scarcely emphasised it, he saw that the simplest clan organisation would be binary: he
cited Australian tribes with moieties, and referred also to Morgan on
North America (*DOL* 150). Clans (or moieties) were simply hordes that
had come together and lost their independence. These qualitatively
similar units could either be juxtaposed in a quasi-linear manner (on
a single level, as we might put it), or, at a higher stage, they could come
together to form hierarchical structures, with groups of clans nested
within one or more higher-order subdivisions of society (*DOL* 153).[4]

Durkheim's thinking shows a certain ambivalence here. Synchronically, he sees clans as ways of segmenting society, but diachronically
they are solidary units, which aggregate to generate new forms. Whatever may have happened in the course of history, his modelling would
have been more economical and self-consistent if he had envisaged
the whole society as the enduring entity, so that new forms arise
diachronically not from aggregation but from segmentation: the horde
splits into moieties, which in turn split into clans, which may or may
not group themselves according to the units from which they originated. Below the level of the clan, Durkheim does envisage fission
rather than fusion (*DOL* 151): the clan in its pure state constitutes a
single family which is undivided and amorphous (*indivise, confuse*), and
it is within this homogeneous mass that individual families separate
out.[5]

Mauss departs from Durkheim, not only in his more consistent
emphasis on fission, but also in giving full weight to exogamy. He spec-
ulates on a prehistoric period with egocentric exogamy (rules prohibiting ego's marriage with close relatives), but what he finds in the
simplest attested societies is sociocentric exogamy (rules prohibiting
ego's marriage within an enduring social unit such as moiety or clan).
Perhaps Durkheim in 1893 missed this point since in North Africa and
the Middle East (to which he refers) clans are not typically exogamous,
as they are elsewhere. In any case, exogamy is fundamental. If an
endogamous society consists of exogamous units, then by definition
the units exchange spouses, in which case their solidarity must consist

in more than the juxtaposition of homogeneous entities sharing a *conscience commune*. There is a division of labour between the unit that provides a person's socio-structural identity (clan membership) and the unit that provides their marriage partner and their children's other parent; and these kinship links must contribute to solidarity.

As to Mauss's other two basic differentiating factors, gender and generation, Durkheim is equally inadequate. He recognises that in a clan-based society such as the Iroquois there are two sexes, but he merely says that 'the adults of the two sexes are the equals of each other' (*DOL* 150); and he claims that kinship is not organised, 'for one cannot give this name [organised kinship] to the distribution of the [social] mass into generational levels', and the obligations uniting a child to its maternal relatives amount to very little.

Durkheim does not confuse relations holding between clans, those aggregates which resemble each other like the segments of an earthworm (*DOL* 150), and relations holding between individuals, who are alike even in skull size, features and character (*DOL* 104–5); but since in both cases the relations are of resemblance, the distinction of levels is unemphatic.[6] Mauss is more explicit, not only in discriminating intra-segment and inter-segment relations (32, III: 13), and also in recognising the crosscutting of the segments by other criteria (34, III: 321–2).

However, in spite of these differentiating factors, Mauss does not entirely discard the notion of amorphism. The idea of society as a homogeneous mass does apply to certain moments of collective life, for instance, as he had shown in 1906, to the social life of Eskimos during winter, when they congregate and live in an atmosphere of ritual (32, III: 14). Thus the homogeneous society and uniform social duration implied by the label 'mechanical solidarity' were both too simple (34, III: 319).[7]

Admittedly, neither the adhesion [of the individual] to society, nor the adhesion of subgroups [to each other] had the same nature as the organic solidarity that Durkheim had defined as characterising modern society, but the problem needed to be complicated. On the one hand, in modern society certain amorphisms [he uses the plural] arise from individualism – we too exhibit mechanical solidarity [voters in a constituency?]. On the other hand there is plenty of organic solidarity in all archaic societies.[8] However it is not the same as ours, which results from contracts, professions and the like. Firstly, it links enduring subgroups, not only individuals, and secondly it does so (I add my glosses) through 'alliances [marital and other], influences [modes of authority] and services [reciprocity], rather than through the presence of supreme authority of the State' [acting via the law].

In fact, Mauss envisaged tribal societies cohering by 'a type of solidarity that is at once mechanical and organic', resulting from the interlacing, crosscutting, or interweaving of different sorts of homogeneities. 'This is how we should represent social cohesion from the earliest times: as mixtures of amorphisms and polymorphisms...amorphisms and polymorphisms do not exclude each other, and reciprocity comes into the picture' (32, III: 18–19). Fundamentally, tribal political life, even tribal social life, was reducible to the articulation (*système d' agencement* 34, III: 320) of the politico-domestic or politico-religious groups. However, as we shall see later, he also takes into account certain individual relationships, notably between ego and grandson.

In the absence of the State, it might seem obscure how order and discipline is maintained between all these crosscutting entities. Mauss does not refer explicitly to Durkheim's *conscience commune* with its penal sanctions, but he may well have it in mind when he talks of 'the sovereignty of the tribe' (32, III: 13). This sovereignty operates in various ways. Thus, there may be recognised rules for the policing of one unit by another, or governing the behaviour of all members of a unit, or allotting authority within it; interactions between units may operate via socialisation (whether deliberate education, or other modes of cultural transmission); and there is often an important explicit ideal of social peace and harmony (ibid.: 24–5, 34, III: 315).

Developing Mauss's ideas

Mauss may seem to have moved a long way from his uncle's thesis but, as he saw it, he was simply making more explicit ideas that were already present (*plus que latentes*) in the work of the pre-war *Année* group (32, III: 13). Indeed he used much the same language as Durkheim, asked similar questions, and related his answers to Durkheim's. Nearly seventy years on, how much further can we take this same line of thought?

One might ask whether new methods have meanwhile emerged for exploring primitive modes of social solidarity. Archaeology, biological anthropology and cognitive sciences such as developmental psychology have obviously progressed, but I doubt if they can offer much help. An essentially new direction of work is the field study of social behaviour among non-human primates. Such species live in groups, and primatologists can tell us about interactions within and between these groups, and even about subgroups within them: thus most primate species possess ranked groups ('matrilines'), while chimpanzees, man's closest relative, with a common ancestry some 5–6 million years back, possess patrilines.

Of course, just as the connection between contemporary tribal peoples and palaeolithic peoples is problematic, so is that between either of these and contemporary chimpanzees. All the same, such connections do get made: for instance, Quiatt and Reynolds (1993: 224–5) suggest continuity of a sort from primate patrilines to the patrilineages of the Kachin as described by Leach (1954). This particular argument leaves me unpersuaded, but one welcomes help from primatologists in thinking about social cohesion among early humans. For instance, Reynolds elsewhere (1974) writes on individual relationships among primates that look very like friendship. Neither Durkheim nor Mauss mention friendship between individuals when discussing social solidarity, but it could well contribute to solidarity.

In any case, much can be done simply with the materials of social anthropology. The method I use here is to try to systematise the ideas that are latent in the work of Mauss. Another method, which gives convergent results and which I have explored elsewhere (Allen 1989a, 1998b), draws on a type of data that Mauss could have used but never did, namely kinship terminologies.[9]

We saw that for Mauss primitive social solidarity arises not only from the homogeneity of individuals or groups in a society, but also from the segmentation of a quasi-homogeneous mass by crosscutting criteria (*clivage en sens divers d'une seule masse d'hommes et de femmes* 1932: 19). He discusses five criteria. The Durkheimian clans with which he starts can be thought of (loosely) as based on affiliation, i.e. on the recruitment of children to the clan of one or other parent; and he goes on to cover locality, sex, age and generation (the final pair differ of course in that an uncle can be younger than his nephew but is always of senior generation). Bearing these criteria in mind, let us now ask what would be the simplest possible model of a human society. The relation between logical simplicity and primitivity in any sense is another contentious issue, but I leave it unargued, and simply press on.

The simplest form of cleavage is clearly a dichotomy, and the fewer the dichotomies we incorporate in the model the simpler it will be. This consideration enables us quickly to eliminate locality. It is easy enough to imagine a society with its territory split in two, or consisting of two mobile residential groups, but this dichotomy is independent of all the others. It could certainly be relevant to solidarity, but to incorporate it is a luxury, which will make the model more complex, not simpler.

Sex and age go together as being inherent in human biology. Sex provides a clear-cut dichotomy for society to use, and indeed Mauss distinguishes men and women within the 'mass' that is to be segmented. Although at first sight age presents itself as a continuum, the biological divide between the immature and those of or past reproductive age makes possible a child-adult dichotomy. But both these dichotomies are available to all societies, and they relate to our question only in so far as sex is subsumed in the notion of affiliation, and age in that of generation.

It is these two remaining criteria that are crucial. Although Mauss treats them respectively first and last (32, III: 13–17), he too regarded them as the irreducible minimum. Thus the 'simplest hypothesis' (*M* 155–6) consists of moieties, patri- or matri-, crosscut by generations, themselves dichotomized by sex. Durkheim, he says (ibid.: 161), did not adequately distinguish the generations within the clan, thereby exaggerating its amorphism; the true amorphism was within generations. Fundamentally, these two criteria go together in that they correspond to the two logically necessary dimensions of kinship systems – the horizontal, pertaining to siblings and spouses, and the vertical, pertaining to parents and children.

Whereas moieties (like sex) necessarily dichotomise, it might seem that generations simply come one after the other, and cannot present the binary simplicity we are looking for. Here, I think, Mauss fails by a whisker to make the crucial observation: biologically speaking, generations form an indefinite sequence, but sociologically, they can very easily be dichotomised. If we follow standard usage and number ego's generation zero, the father's and sons's +1 and -1, the grandfather's and grandson's +2 and -2, and so on, then the generations can be dichotomised into even-numbered and odd-numbered. Provided it prohibits marriage between even- and odd-numbered generations, there is nothing to stop a society splitting itself in this way.

Mauss surely knows that Australian four-section systems ('marriage class systems', as he calls them) in effect do just this. Figures 3.1 and 3.2 show the essentials of a four-section system. Each section (A–D) contains males and females linked internally by classificatory siblingship,[10] and each section is linked to others by relations of affiliation and marriage (note that the model prohibits a male ego from marrying not only his sister, but also his mother or daughter).

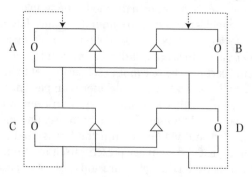

Figure 3.1 Four-section system in traditional genealogical notation

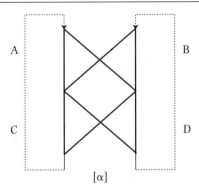

[α]

Figure 3.2 As Figure 3.1, in the improved notation developed by Héran (1996).

Notes: In the latter, opposite-sex siblings are shown, not by a triangle and a circle joined by a horizontal line a little above them, but by a vertical and oblique line diverging from their tops, while spouses are shown by lines converging at their bottoms and pointing down to their children. The [α] indicates that it is immaterial which sex is allocated to vertical lines and which to oblique. In both diagrams same-sex siblingship is treated as identity, and the broken lines indicate the repetition of relationships after two generations.

Durkheim and Mauss (1903) take the Australian systems as their starting point in *PC* (cf. Ch. 2), and both in 1932 and elsewhere (*M* 172), Mauss says that similar systems are widespread among tribal populations outside Australia.[11] Moreover, when connecting solidarity and reciprocity, he mentions the common phenomenon of termino-logical equation of a grandfather and his grandson (as if in English each addressed the other as 'male grand-relative'); he even talks of their 'identity', recognising how they may stand together in opposition to the intervening male relative (32 III 19). If he had brought all these points together, he would have formulated the model we are looking for. In terms of segmentation, it simply crosscuts a generation-based dichotomy of society with an affiliation-based dichotomy. In terms of solidarity, it generates cohesion by using parent-child relationships as well as marital alliances.

Mauss's thinking and the proposed revision

It is interesting to ask why Mauss never quite spelled out what was implicit in his various formulations. One obstacle may have been the way in which he divided up the field of sociology. Solidarity, as we noted, concerned the segmentation of society as a whole and belonged to general sociology, while kinship he saw primarily as a juridical phenomenon. Although in practice he tends to relate the two topics, he does not sufficiently emphasise that in a small-scale society all members may be counted as relatives, so that the segmentation of society into enduring units and the classification of relatives into egocentric categories can operate on the same mass of males and females. Hence he did not pose the question of whether and how the two forms of structuring could be congruent.

Secondly, he may have retained Durkheim's view that sections arose historically from an original matrimoiety structure crosscut by later patrimoieties, a view he endorsed in 1907 (II: 432). As a matter of logic, a society with four sections embodies three dichotomies (apart from males versus females): A+C versus B+D (matrimoieties), A+D versus B+C (patrimoieties), and A+B versus C+D (generation moieties). Any two of these imply the third. Because in the Australian case he was thinking of the two affiliation-based moieties, he perhaps did not sufficiently attend to the generation moieties.

A third problem concerns reciprocity, a theme that he related both to the horizontal and the vertical dimensions of kinship. Horizontally, he spoke of enduring intergroup relations and transgenerational expectations relating to marital alliance (34, III: 320–1), and in his lists of what is exchanged in systems of total prestations he included women.[12] Vertically, he talks of simple or direct reciprocity between different generations (32, III: 19), and also of indirect reciprocity such as is more familiar to us (I give to my son what he gives to his M 130); but in both cases he is thinking of the egocentric domain, i.e. of relatives.[13] Although he includes children in his lists of total prestations, I now think (cf. Allen 1989b: 48 n2) that he had in mind either indirect reciprocity or the horizontal exchange of children for fostering, and that he never conceptualised the relation of A+B to C+D as one of direct reciprocity. However, that is what it is. Children produced by one generation moiety are given to the other to constitute its membership, and the prestation is reciprocated. When discussing reincarnation and the notion of the person, he was perfectly aware of the identification of individuals in alternate generations, but he does not connect this idea with his understanding of total prestations and inter-group reciprocity.

Whatever the reasons for his lack of synthesis, Mauss, building on Durkheim, provides all that is needed for the starting point of an evolutionary theory of social structures and kinship systems. I have put forward this theory elsewhere (1986, 1989a), calling it 'tetradic' to emphasise precisely the crosscutting of at least two social dichotomies (the biological distinction of males versus females being taken for granted).

Contrary to Mauss, and even more to Durkheim, I give theoretical primacy not to the sex-specific affiliation-based dichotomies with their horizontal exchanges, but to the sex-neutral generational dichotomy with its child exchange. Since any two of the dichotomies imply the third, the choice may not be crucial, but if the generational one is as important as Mauss thought, it is best to build it in explicitly from the start. The other model-building possibilities, none of them particularly tempting, are (i) to envisage the generational dichotomy as the by-product of the two affiliations; (ii) to take one affiliation dichotomy (but how is it to be chosen?), and then cross-cut it by generation; (iii) to move in one step from undivided horde to quadripartition. But perhaps the best justification for my priority lies in the very notion of society. To endure, a society must produce successive generations, and this *ipso facto* necessitates a division of labour: those of reproductive age have to produce the next generation, but not the generation after next. Here are two tasks, which have to be performed by society, but cannot be performed by the same group.

But why should there only be two groups? Two is of course the logical minimum, but there may be a biological factor too, one which takes us back to Mauss's inclusion of age among the fundamental segmenting factors. As producer of the next generation, I will be replaced by my son, as he will be by his; but as member of society, the chances are that my life-span largely overlaps with my son's, and that in this capacity I will be replaced by my grandson. The average life span lasts about two generations. Mauss does not ask why the identification of ego and great-grandson is empirically so rare, but perhaps the generation/life-span ratio supplements the logical minimum argument.

Mechanical solidarity revisited

In conclusion, let us return to the horde. Mauss used the idea chiefly as a tool for thinking about periods of social concentration and effervescence (compare Turner's notion of communitas – 1969: 80 ff.); but something like an endogamous horde is also a necessary starting point for model-building. If we are to talk of segmentation, we need a totality to segment, and in spite of contemporary attacks on the notion of social or tribal boundedness (which are often perfectly well grounded in contemporary ethnography), I suppose that for most of its history humanity has lived in societies each having a fairly clear sense of its social boundary. Mauss was very well aware that societies were not watertight: he and Durkheim discussed higher levels of social organisation in the last pre-War *Année* (13, II: 451–5), and he frequently reverted to similar diffusionist points about 'civilisational areas'.

Nevertheless, he also emphasised the discreteness of many societies. A society has a name, borders, a desire to think of itself as distinct from outsiders, a sense of itself as a totality within which peace should reign, and often a belief in common origin (34, III: 314 f.). The two enduring features of a society are its territory and, even more so, its *constitution* (10, III: 377).

This raises again the question of the non-human primates. Do they exhibit anything like a bounded society with crosscutting segmentation? My limited knowledge suggests not. The co-resident group exports one sex of offspring when they become sexually mature (females in the chimpanzee case), but the recipient groups plus home group do not seem to constitute a demographic isolate resembling an endogamous society. If not, and if we assume that the common ancestors were chimpanzee-like as regards social solidarity, then the transition to humanity involved quantum changes difficult to reconcile with any sort of continuity from primate patrilines to Kachin patrilineages. My hypothesis, again in the Durkheimian tradition, is that the transition involved the invention of ritual, and patterned sexual coupling in the context of ritual (Allen 1982 and Ch. 4).[14]

At any rate, I hope to have shown that, although Durkheim's characterisation of primitive social solidarity is unsatisfactory in several ways, his approach is still useful. We do indeed need to start, not from individuals who are linked, but from society as an endogamous totality that is segmented. By enriching Durkheim's exclusive emphasis on affiliation-based segmentation with Mauss's interest in generations, we can produce a model of primitive society which both accords with the simplest possible mode of classifying relatives and is not world-historically implausible.

In the light of this model the notion of mechanical solidarity takes on new aspects. In the most general sense, all the members of society are linked to each other as relatives. It is this relatedness that holds society together, both at the level of groups and individuals. All participate in the same cohesive structure, and their shared participation constitutes a resemblance. Crudely: mechanical solidarity equals kinship.

To be sure, this generalised homogeneity resolves itself into a series of different relations. The structure can be looked at in terms of segmentation (sociocentrically) or in terms of egos and alters (egocentrically), and as quadripartite (ignoring sex) or eight-element (including sex); and sex itself can be thought of in relative terms (sex *a* versus sex *b*, however *a* and *b* are allocated) or in absolute terms (male versus female). Nevertheless, except in the last case, we never encounter in the model absolute differences such as characterise different occupations under organic solidarity: one section has exactly the same properties as another, one ego is situated within the whole exactly like any other ego. From this point of view the society really is founded on similarities.

One can go a little further. The model is an expression of certain rules of marriage and recruitment, and a corresponding society could only work if the rules were generally recognised. Suppose we label this general recognition *conscience commune*. Would it then be unreasonable to imagine our distant ancestors using repressive sanctions against deviants?

Notes

1. Of the 150 authors he refers to (Borlandi 1993: 67–70), barely half a dozen might qualify as ethnographers, and he relies heavily on compilers such as Waitz.
2. If these papers are all from the second half of Mauss's career, it is no doubt because in the first half he concentrated on religion, leaving the area of kinship to his uncle. With Durkheim dead, he tried to stand in for him and cover the whole of *sociologie*.
3. Compare his own interest in 'total social facts'. More generally, if at this period Mauss was preoccupied with establishing the 'shape' of the discipline, it was partly because he was trying to carry forward Durkheim's effort to establish its existence. For those who teach it, this problem of 'shape' has by no means disappeared.
4. According to Wallwork (1984) Durkheim recognised six stages of social evolution.
5. Durkheim suggests two names for his post-horde model of primitive society: segmentary societies with a clan basis, and societies with a politico-familial organisation. He prefers the former as emphasising what gives these societies their characteristic structure (*structure propre*) (*DOL* 151–2).
6. The very notion of 'level', seemingly indispensable in contemporary academic discourse, in scarcely to be found in the relevant sense in the works of Durkheim and Mauss.
7. This must have become clear to Durkheim, as well as Mauss, by the time of *PC* in 1903. I think the demonstration that, internally, primitive categories tend to be more sharply differentiated and less homogeneous than modern ones is among the most important achievements of the *Année* school (Ch. 1 above).
8. He regards the 'really primitive' Australians as a possible exception. I do not understand why, since it might be argued that by linking units of society with departments of nature Australian totemism offered a particularly clear form of the division of ritual labour.
9. Though of course well aware of Morgan's work on the subject, he did not discuss it at length. Reporting on his teaching for 1903–4 (III: 73), he mentions the 'remarkable' reanalyses by his student Chaillié of Morgan's data on two Eskimo terminologies. [No doubt he builds on these analyses in his *Seasonal Variations* (06 SA 451), where he notes traces of Morgan's classificatory type in the terminological equations of the ± 2 genealogical level.]
10. Classificatory siblings are those whom ego classifies as siblings. To work out what relatives will be so classified one uses the principle of equivalence of same-sex siblings. Since ego's father and ego's father's brother are same-sex siblings they are equivalent, and therefore a father's brother's son (to us a cousin) is like a father's son, in other words he is a classificatory brother. The principle applies generally, and explains why each quadrant of the diagram needs only one male and one female

symbol – the symbols cover innumerable relatives of different degrees of remoteness. Ch. 4 also presents four-section systems, and complements these brief remarks.

11. Though he does not say this, the instances he was thinking of from outside Australia would have lacked section names, the sections being simply implicit in the kinship system.

12. These were points developed by 'alliance theorists' in the social anthropology of the 1950s and '60s.

13. It is no doubt this indirect reciprocity that he has in mind in his 1931 discussion with Piaget (III: 301).

14. Goldschmidt claims (1993: 345) that 'the invention of ritual was as crucial as was that of language to the development of culture.' For the development of solidarity it may have been even more crucial.

Chapter 4

EFFERVESCENCE AND THE ORIGINS OF HUMAN SOCIETY

There are many reasons why one might be interested in *Elementary Forms*, but mine may not be among the most obvious: I am interested in the origins of human society, and think that the great classic can help us reflect on how society acquired a structure. This does not imply blanket endorsement – I shall also have some criticisms of the work; but my aim is less to identify defects than to look for help in answering unsolved questions.

At first sight it may seem unlikely that the book can be used in this way. Surely, one might think, what Durkheim has to say about social origins must be wholly out of date, both as regards theory and facts? Has not social anthropology long ago rejected the evolutionism that Durkheim took for granted, and do we not nowadays know so much more than he did about prehistory, let alone about Australian Aborigines?

However, neither issue is straightforward. Take the matter of theories. It is perfectly true that, within social anthropology, soon after Durkheim's time there was a massive rejection of evolutionism, and that, in spite of protests from Marxists and others, the whole approach remains somewhat out of favour. No doubt, Durkheim did underestimate the problems of moving from nineteenth-century tribal ethnography to the social history of mankind fifty or more millennia earlier. On the other hand, it is not clear what it means to 'reject evolutionism'. The phrase can merely imply that social anthropologists should get on with their fieldwork and not waste time speculating about the distant past. Such pragmatically based rejection no doubt served a useful function in the growth of the discipline, and remains a reasonable position for individuals to adopt; but there is no reason why it should still constrain the curiosity of all practitioners. Rejection of evolutionism can also mean avoiding certain vocabulary, words like 'primitive' and 'progress', which sound dated and may be taken to imply unacceptable value judgements; but a rejection based on such politico-moral-aesthetic grounds is quite different from one based on theoretical or epistemological grounds.

In its strictest form this third sort of rejection (the most interesting) would maintain that ethnography is of zero relevance to world history – either because the latter concept is itself incoherent, or because the relevance is too difficult, or even impossible, to establish: societies simply cannot be allotted to stages allowing systematic comparison between different periods. But an argument along these lines puts one on a slippery slope: carried through consistently, it has to deny that one social group can ever be classified as moving ahead of or falling behind another with respect to any particular feature – an extreme and untenable stance. Like any other approach, evolutionism can be misused; but practised with sufficient skill and caution, it is not an unreasonable means of trying to understand society, and the fact that Durkheim was an evolutionist does not in itself render his ideas obsolete.

I turn next to Durkheim's data. Clearly the range of facts on which *Elementary Forms* draws is very limited. The book is about the origin of religion, and Durkheim holds that most social institutions derive from religion; so he is really dealing with the origin of sociality, of human society as we know it. This situates his undertaking in what would now be called palaeoanthropology. However, this latter has become a huge subject drawing on specialities such as primatology, molecular genetics, sociobiology, palaeontology, climatology, ecology, archaeology, psychology and linguistics, not to mention social anthropology (see e.g., Mellars and Stringer 1989). Its biological component covers such matters as bipedalism, encephalisation, infantile dependency, reproductive physiology and vocal tract anatomy; but it also deals with technology (use of fire, stone tools, figurines, rock art), and with more sociological topics such as the sexual division of labour (between males who mainly hunt and females who mainly gather), and the use of resources (non-humans tend to consume food where they find it, humans take it to a base and share it). The picture is enriched by theories of mental evolution, of the development and reabsorption of specialised cognitive domains or modules (Mithen 1996). The topics are interlinked in complex ways, and the whole story is given a measure of precision by scientific dating techniques. If one situates *Elementary Forms* in this context, it does seem unlikely that, after more than eighty years, it should still have something to offer. But unlikely though it be, that is what I argue.

I shall try to show that the Durkheimian notion of effervescence goes some way towards answering one of the fundamental questions about social origins. It is a question that at first sight pertains more to the domain of kinship and social structure than to religion, but for Durkheim the two are not wholly separate: religion, like so much of human culture, goes back to clan assemblies. Such assemblies generate effervescence, a state in which clan members become aware of forces transcending the individual. Responding creatively to these forces, they symbolise them with totemic emblems, thereby originating the category of the sacred. For initiation rituals the tribe as a whole assembles, generating even more transcendent sacred concepts.

My central concern is not with the sacred or with totemic concepts, but with the context in which they supposedly develop, namely with the 'effervescent assembly' (Pickering 1984). Although I do not know the palaeoanthropological literature in any depth, I doubt if it often refers to such assemblies; for instance they do not feature in the work even of someone such as Knight (1991; Knight et al. 1995), who starts from a social anthropological background. But why do they merit attention? To answer this question, I consider first the simplest ways of organising a primitive small-scale society, and then ask how such an organisation might itself arise.

Truly elementary social structures

Organisation implies division into units or categories. Biology provides two obvious bases for division, namely sex and age, but any further division must be based on social rules. All sorts of rules are theoretically conceivable, for instance a lottery that allocates individuals to groups at some point or points in their life-span. In practice, however, societies seldom employ chance for such fundamental purposes, and the general experience of anthropologists strongly suggests that the earliest human sociostructural rules related to kinship and marriage. This is a classical topic for anthropological theorising, and for some years I have been interested in the simplest way of combining the relevant variables. The solution is a type of structure that I call 'tetradic', since it is quadripartite. However, the way in which tetradic structures themselves originated is less clear, and it is here that the effervescent assembly comes to the rescue.

I must now summarise certain features of tetradic theory (Allen 1986; 1989a). It will be a few pages before I return explicitly to the assemblies, but I shall be dealing with matters on which Durkheim wrote elsewhere (especially 1898) and which are highly relevant to EF.

There are several ways of introducing tetradic models. One approach starts with disciplinary history and presents the theory as the logical development of previous attempts in the same direction. A second starts with data on attested societies, chooses the simplest, and tries to simplify yet further. A third works deductively, starting from first principles. In addition, one must opt whether to look at the rules of kinship and marriage from outside (how they structure society as a whole) or from inside (how they bear on an individual ego who has relatives to classify). I was led to tetradic theory largely by an inductive and egocentric path, but here, as in Chapter 3 (this volume), I take a deductive and sociocentric approach.

So let us start from first principles, and envisage society as an enduring and demographically bounded whole, replenishing itself by its own reproductive activity – the 'structureless horde' of Durkheim's earlier writings. This constitutes a totality, 'the category par excellence' as Durkheim calls it (*EF*: 609). The society contains males and females, young and old, but how else could it be structured? The simplest answer is by bisection into two halves or moieties on the basis of generation. If one moiety is A, the other B, we stipulate that each is endogamous: members of A always and only marry other members of A, and their children belong to B. Members of B marry each other, and *their* children belong to A.

In other words the two moieties exchange children: individuals born in the wombs of A are given to B to constitute its membership, and vice versa. If I am in A, my children and parents are in B, my grandrelatives are in A, my great-grand-relatives in B, and so on.[1] Since generations are conventionally shown horizontally, one can diagram thus:

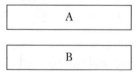

It is important to see that the distribution of ages is the same in each moiety. It is not the case that moiety A contains my contemporaries and those of my grandrelatives, moiety B those of my parents and children. The mistake is easily made because of the ambiguity of the English word 'generation', which means both 'contemporaries' and 'genealogical level'. In fact, moving away from ego to remoter and remoter cousins, one finds within A individuals of all ages, none of them more representative than any other. Generation moieties are not particularly odd, anthropologically speaking. I first met them in a classic essay by Hocart (1970:177) concerning the hill tribes of one of the islands of Fiji: 'the whole population is divided into two alternate generations called *tako* and *lavo* . . .'

An alternative way of bisecting a society on the basis of rules of kinship and marriage is into descent moieties, which are conventionally shown vertically:

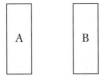

In this case, the moieties are exogamous, so that members of A must marry in B and vice versa. In terms of exchange the two units can be thought of as swapping nubile women, not children. However, this marriage rule says nothing about recruitment. Consider a male in A: we need to specify whether his children belong in A or B. The options give respectively patrimoieties and matrimoieties.

We are now in a position to envisage the most obvious tetradic models. They arise if generation moieties are crosscut by descent moieties. Each generation moiety remains endogamous, but it is subdivided into exogamous 'sections', as they are nowadays called. One diagrams thus:

The horizontal relations are easy to envisage, but a slightly more subtle point concerns the vertical dimension. It might seem that the descent moieties need to be specified as either patri- or matri-, but in fact the choice is unnecessary. This is because four entities, whether sections or anything else, can be generated by two crosscutting dichotomies of an initial totality, but they can then be arranged in three pairs: ab/cd, ac/bd, ad/bc. So the four sections produced by crosscutting generation moieties with patrimoieties can be rearranged on the page or in the mind (of native or analyst) as matrimoieties, and vice versa if the cross-cutting is with matrimoieties. Given two of the dichotomies the third is implicit.

This point is close to Durkheim's interests. Four-section systems are of course extremely widespread in Australia, and he discussed them in *EF* and elsewhere, albeit using different vocabulary – *classe matrimoniale* for 'section' and *phratrie* for 'moiety'. He envisaged them as resulting from primal matrimoieties cross-cut by patrilocal residence, i.e., in effect as the product of the two types of descent moieties. My own emphasis on generation moieties derives from the significance I attach to child exchange, as will become clear at the end of this chapter.

So far, the tetradic model has been presented in sociocentric terms, as a way of structuring a self-reproducing population. But that gives only a partial view, for the model also needs to be understood egocentrically. This means locating ego in one of the sections and working out the distribution of ego's relatives. Given the built-in rules of marriage and recruitment, it is an easy logical exercise: provided the rules are followed, all possible relatives fall into one or other section. Genealogical distance makes no difference. Whether long dead, or not yet born, all have their place (see figures 3.1 and 3.2).

In other words, the four sections of society are precisely congruent with four categories of relatives. Society, doubly dichotomised, and the domain of relatives, arranged in four categories, are coextensive, and use the same dividing lines.[2] The difference consists merely in the point of view, in the way units are identified. Sections can be named, in the ordinary sense of the word 'named', whereas categories of relative can only be identified relative to ego, by a kinship term. The four units can be labelled in these two different ways. That is why the analyst can approach tetradic models equally well by a sociocentric or egocentric route.

As I have discussed elsewhere (1998b), there are many tetradic structures other than the one just presented, but I should emphasise that all are hypothetical. Four-section systems exist ethnographically, as I mentioned, but the associated classification of relatives is always more complex than in the model. If (to simplify) kinship terminology and classification of relatives are taken as synonymous, one always finds more than four kinship terms – indeed more than the eight that would result from splitting the four according to sex. Thus the Kariera of north-west Australia, the text-book example of a four-section system, had around twenty terms. Nevertheless, logically speaking, four would suffice to form a coherent system and one that is not very remote from human practice as we know it.

Why cannot the reduction be carried further? Why would a single dichotomy, accompanied by a binary division of relatives, fail to accord with what is characteristically human? Whichever of the three dichotomies one chooses, the classification would simply divide relatives into those of ego's moiety and those of the other. What is wrong with that?

The problem becomes clear when one relates marriage rules to incest. Incest is a fundamental topic, long debated by anthropologists. For many, including Malinowski (1927: 179) and Lévi-Strauss, it stands on the border between nature and culture, between non-human and human, and I take it as evidence of Durkheim's anthropological insight that he chose it as the subject for what was both his first original text focusing on tribal societies and the opening article in the first volume of the *Année sociologique* (1898).

Notions of incest are culturally variable, but for analysts the term usually refers simply to the (almost universal) prohibition of sexual intercourse between close relatives, and particularly between primary relatives, i.e., members of the nuclear family. In this minimal sense there are two sorts of incest, intra-generational between brother and sister, and inter-generational between parent and child (either mother-son or father-daughter). Of course sexual intercourse – which can be intra- or extra-marital – and marriage – which may or may not involve intercourse – are not synonymous. All the same, marriage can normally be taken to imply intercourse, and the simplest arrangement is for the rules governing marriage also to govern intercourse, so that sex is prohibited outside marriage.

The central point is that a single dichotomy of society cannot rule out incest of both sorts. A division into generation moieties leaves open brother-sister marriage; matrimoieties leave open father-daughter marriage; and patrimoieties leave open mother-son marriage. It might seem that the last two could be avoided by stipulating change of moiety membership on marriage: a woman would join her husband's patrimoiety, and hence (for instance if she were widowed) be ruled out as a legitimate partner for her son. But the problem is merely relocated: a change applying to the mother at her marriage must apply to her daughter at hers, so that after her marriage the latter becomes a legitimate partner for her own father. To rule out both horizontal and vertical forms of incest one needs two dichotomies.

It is worth translating this sociocentric argument into egocentric terms. It is widely known that tribal peoples tend to group relatives into categories containing indefinite numbers of what to us seem wholly different types of relative. The discovery of 'classificatory' kinship terminologies goes back to Morgan in 1871, and has been described as 'the single most important ethnographic breakthrough of all time' (Barnard 1994: 803). So could not the earliest kinship terminologies have consisted of terms grouping all relatives within a moiety? But consider the consequences. Under generation moieties a woman classes in her own moiety her husband and brother; under matrimoieties she classes together in the opposite moiety her husband and father; under patrimoieties her husband and son. In other words she systematically conflates marriageable and unmarriageable: a two-term terminology fails to make the conceptual distinctions needed to avoid marriage within the nuclear family. A four-term terminology does just that: a woman's father, brother and son are located in three of the categories while the fourth, the source of her husband, contains no primary relatives until she marries into it.

A tetradic terminology, though logically neater and more consistent than any in the ethnographic record, makes no use of principles that

are not attested. The classification of all relatives of a given genealogical level under two heads (which may be subdivided by sex and relative age) is commonplace, and the grouping together of relatives from
alternate genealogical levels is by no means rare. On a scale leading
from empty theoretical simplicity to attested complexity, quadripartition represents a breakthrough, an ethnographic Rubicon.

Australia

Having introduced what I take to be the simplest structuring of society
that would look human, I turn to the question of Durkheim's choice of
Australia. I have referred twice to Aboriginal data, but this was largely
in the hope of retaining the interest of those who find kinship somewhat abstract and dry, and not at all because the argument depended
on Australian data. It is a fact of logic that if one tries to model a society in which everyone is related to everyone else, and to do so using
rules of kinship and marriage and taking account of the minimal
incest prohibitions, then a quadripartite model is the simplest possible.
This would be just as true if measles or some other scourge had wiped
out all Aborigines before a line of ethnography had been written on
them. That said, however, it is interesting that Australia offers forms of
social organisation closer to tetradic models than other areas of the
world, insofar as such closeness can be estimated. There is one
instance of a four-section system reported from south-eastern Peru
(Kensinger 1985), and the system has sometimes been postulated as
underlying attested forms elsewhere; but Australia remains its *locus
classicus* – reports go back at least to the 1850s (Needham 1974: 118).
The coincidence is interesting because on page 1 of *Elementary Forms*
Durkheim announces that he is seeking societies of maximal organi-
sational simplicity; similarly, he claims later (*EF*: 136) that the organisation of the Australian tribes is the most primitive and simple that is
known. Ironically however, he mislocates this simplicity: instead of
associating it with the four-section systems, he locates it in the organisation by clans (ibid.). In other words, he overlooks horizontal splitting, based on child exchange, and theorises solely in terms of vertical
splitting; indeed he thinks the clans arise from vertical splitting of the
primal matrimoieties, which themselves arise from splitting of the
original 'compact and undivided mass' (1898: 63). Perhaps he was
influenced by the greater frequency of descent-based constructs
throughout the ethnographic world, or by their prominence in the Biblical and classical worlds (the first 'alien' cultures that he knew much
about), or by Robertson Smith. But whatever the explanation, he was
seeking sociostructural simplicity in the right ethnographic region.

For other reasons too, his choice of Australia is less arbitrary than critics often suppose. He refers briefly to the technology as *rudimentaire* and to the absence of houses or even huts (*EF*: 136), also to the 'hunting-fishing' economy (*EF*: 334), but there is nowadays more to be said. Australia offers one of the very few large areas of the world where the population continued to rely exclusively on hunting and gathering right up until the time when ethnographers began to describe them; and not only that, but it was populated at an early date (60,000–40,000 B.C., tens of millennia before the New World, let alone the Arctic), and thereafter it had little cultural or demographic exchange with the rest of the world. Relative isolation plus conservatism in technology and mode of subsistence does not necessarily imply conservatism in other cultural domains such as social structure or religion; but in assessing Durkheim's undertaking, the special position of Australia on the ethnographic world map is worth remembering.

However, if tetradic theory is right, and if one is looking to totemic social structure to explain the earliest forms of religion, then one ought to look, not to totemic clans, but to totemic sections. Durkheim refers to the possibility of tribes having section totems (*EF*: 154–55), but he gives them little weight. In 1903 he and Mauss had treated classifications based on four sections (such as the Wakelbura) before those based on clans, but I doubt if this implied some shadowy sense of the evolutionary priority of sections; it was simply that they were moving from binary via quadripartite classifications to ones with larger numbers of units. In any case, the difference between clan and section merely concerns mode of recruitment: a section contains neither of ego's parents, a clan contains one of them and a caste or endogamous stratum contains both.[3] But the mode of recruitment to a group has no bearing on the idea that, when it assembles, its members become aware of forces transcending the individual, and my criticism of Durkheim's treatment of sections leaves unaffected what he says about effervescence.

Gatherings

Apart from clan versus section, there is another unsatisfying aspect of Durkheim's argument, namely the weight he gives to clan rituals (the *intichiuma*) relative to the tribal rituals of initiation. He treats the former first and at greater length, and leaves the reader feeling that they are chronologically prior. No doubt he does this because he regards the totemic emblems as the first sacred symbols, and wants to interpret the high gods such as Baiame and Daramulun, worshipped exclusively

at the tribal gatherings, as pointing to higher stages of religious evolution (*EF*: 420). But there is a difficulty here. As he realises (*EF*: 221,
335n), totemic organisation necessarily implies a degree of coordination between clans, if only to prevent them adopting identical totems.
But how could such coordination be effected except at tribal gatherings? The totemic clan presupposes the tribal assembly, which is therefore logically prior.[4] Should not Durkheim have put the emphasis on
tribal ritual rather than on clan ritual?

If he had, this too would leave the concept of effervescence unaffected. The larger gathering could generate ideas of the sacred as well
as or better than the smaller. Indeed, the argument would become
more characteristically Durkheimian, for in so far as a clan is exogamous, it can never be more than part of a society, while Durkheim
usually emphasises society as a whole – if not as *the* whole. But it does
not follow that a tribal gathering would have to generate a unitary
sacred concept like a high god. A gathering that emphasised social
quadripartition could generate a fourfold idea of the sacred.

In thinking about tribal assemblies among hunter-gatherers
(whether ethnographic or prehistoric), I suspect Durkheim was right
to emphasise the emotions generated simply by assembling. I have felt
something similar, and noted it in others, even in a peasant society.
The days pass in the more or less humdrum activities of village life,
with social contacts confined to a small circle of relatives and neighbours and a gathering such as a festival or market does indeed produce
excitement. Probably everyone has had similar experiences, and the
effect may be greater in hunter-gatherer society, where the population
density is typically so low and the membership of the coresidential
band so restricted (of the order of twenty-five members).

Let me insert a note on the history of ideas. Pickering notes (1984:
382) that Durkheim himself used the term 'effervescence' in *Suicide* in
1897 and in other writings from around 1900, but suggests that in *EF*
Durkheim was also drawing on the famous 1906 essay by Mauss on
the Eskimos. This is certainly right, and it merits more attention than
it usually receives. Mauss too, was studying hunter-gatherers, and dis-
tinguishing between two phases of social life, dispersed nomadism
during the summer, when religious activity is minimal, and concentration in the winter stations, where life is given over to religion and
sociability. Mauss actually uses the term effervescence in describing
the phase when his tribal society is concentrated (*SA*: 470), and a close
comparison between the two texts would show that not only vocabulary but also many of the fundamental ideas of *EF* are foreshadowed
in 1906. No doubt Mauss in turn was partly drawing on his uncle, but
Durkheim's two footnote references to his nephew's paper are scanty
acknowledgement.[5]

To return to my main theme – according to Durkheim, gatherings are creative in that they are the social context in which religion originates; but at the same time, under totemism, the relation between religion and social structure is so close that the two are virtually aspects of each other (thus he derives incest prohibitions from the exogamy of totemic clans). So should we envisage both religion and kinship-based social structure arising in the same context?

The main attraction of this idea is the implausibility of alternatives, and in particular the difficulty of imagining how a tetradic structure could arise among hunter-gatherers dispersed in bands over considerable areas of countryside. The classification of ego's relatives, the positive rules of recruitment and marriage, the negative rules against incest, the division of society into units – all are interlinked, and although the package is not complicated (indeed it is logically as simple as one can get), it does presuppose a conception of society as a totality. How could the whole complex originate except when the whole society (or at least its representatives) was assembled in one place? [6]

Palaeoanthropology usually sees matters differently, giving each aspect of primitive society a separate origin story. Thus social structure may be derived from two hordes, which meet and decide to exchange females; or the minimal lineages, which in chimpanzees link the patrilineal descendants of a patriarch, are envisaged as expanding in time and scope so as to cover the descendants of a dead clan founder. [7] As for incest, many (e.g., Fox 1980) start with the avoidance of close kin mating in apes, and envisage it turning into a sanctioned rule and expanding its range until in some societies it becomes the rule of clan exogamy. Similarly, the usual approach to the origin of classificatory kinship terminologies, for instance that of Morgan himself, or of Fortes (1983: 21, citing Radcliffe-Brown), envisages the terminology starting off with primary relatives and creeping outwards to meet the sociocentric divides. Such approaches can be called 'extensionist', in that they take the individual as the starting point for theorising and work outwards; some writers of this persuasion explicitly dissociate themselves from Durkheim, who is presented as an outdated functionalist. In contrast, my own approach, which follows both Durkheim and Hocart, aims to be consistently contractionist. No doubt extensionism can be useful for purely synchronic purposes, but I think that the less explored contractionist view is closer to what actually happened and has more insights to offer.

Origins

Returning to effervescent assemblies, one need not regard them as a distinctively human innovation. On the contrary, primatological descriptions of 'chimp carnivals' suggest a pre-human origin, which may indeed go back many millions of years (Reynolds 1967: 106–7). What happens is that groups of apes from different areas meet, perhaps at places where food is abundant, and the meeting results in 'social excitement'. Individuals shake branches, fling themselves around in trees, jump up and down, bang the ground or drum on trees (particularly on the thin protrusions that fan out at the base of certain species), vocalise loudly and sometimes rhythmically or in chorus (ibid.: 131–32, 181). The occasions may stimulate sexual activity (ibid.: 107, 123), and Reynolds compares them in passing with the festivities of hunter-gatherers (ibid.: 271). So the contrast between periods of social dispersal and concentration seems to have extremely deep roots.[8]

If tetradic structures originated during the gatherings, the dispersed phase of social life might for a while have continued to operate according to older patterns. Instantaneous spread of the innovation from the one social context to the other seems less likely than a transitional period juxtaposing old and new.

Effervescent assemblies, chimp or human, tend to involve sexual behaviour, but it does not follow that the regulation of this behaviour was the original reason for the emergence of a tetradic structure. Apart from sex the assemblies involve other behaviour potentially subject to structuring. Is it not more likely that creativity and experimentation were directed in the first instance to aesthetic or ludic ends, rather than to social engineering? Various possibilities might be considered – chanting, drumming, dancing, ritual role-playing, games or contests. Durkheim himself remarks on the 'recreational' aspects of ritual (*EF*: 542–43), and there is no need here to be more specific.

However, I have long wondered (Allen 1982) whether the innovation might be related to the notion of rhythm – a topic mentioned in connection with gatherings by Reynolds, Mauss and Durkheim.[9] Rhythm involves repetitions (of sound, movement or whatever), and can of course be generated by a single individual or a chorus acting in concert. But an alternative is for more than one individual or group to take turns. So perhaps the original function of the dichotomies (or an early one) was to structure the 'recreation' by group turn-taking.

Let us then imagine the gathering splitting into four teams or dance groups, which pattern the subsequent sexual relations. If the pattern was carried over from one gathering to the next, that might go some way towards explaining the tetradic marriage rules, but it would say nothing about recruitment. New members of society are born (whether from relations during the gatherings or during the phase of dispersal), and they have to be placed somewhere within the quadripartite whole. But how? Does Durkheim offer any hints?

I think he does, though not deliberately. As we noted, he said that the purpose of the tribal gatherings was initiation, but he did not explain why that ritual should occur at tribal rather than clan gatherings, or indeed why it is so salient in Australian and other ethnography (La Fontaine 1985). But initiation and recruitment both concern the continuity of society across the generations, so they could be linked.

My suggestion is that originally initiation was not into the clan of the relevant parent but into the opposite generation moiety, or a section of it. In other words, child exchange took place not at birth but at initiation: what I called a generation moiety actually contained individuals belonging to two generations – initiated members of one, and uninitiated members of the next. Another way of putting it would be to define a generation as stetching, not from birth to childbirth within one life-span, but from initiation to initiation across two. The idea has various attractions.

1. Empirically, in tribal ethnography generally, birth ritual is much less salient than initiation, which tends to occur shortly before reproductive maturity. Although in the archaeological record initiation is less salient than death ritual, it is not necessarily less ancient or less fundamental.
2. Where perinatal mortality is high, the continuity of society is ensured less by the birth of babies (which is merely the precondition for there being a generation after next) than by their arrival at reproductive maturity. If rites are 'above all the ways by which groups periodically affirm themselves' (*EF*: 553), initiation is the most sensible time in the life-cycle at which to affirm the enduring existence of the group, whether the group in question is society or its sections.
3. If horizontal marital exchange is dramatised by weddings, presumably vertical child exchange should have been dramatised no less forcefully; and whatever may be its functions in attested societies, initiation could have served that purpose in a tetradic society. One might go further. If initiation and wedding were once parts of a single ritual complex, then, by dramatising both of the fundamental modes of exchange at the same time, the ritual could have provided a perfect instance of a system of *prestations totales* – better than any that Mauss could have found in the ethnographic literature.

Further questions

Many issues have been left undiscussed. Assuming tetradic theory is right, did the structure emerge just once, or did it emerge repeatedly at different times and places? Is there any possibility of dating the emergence, either absolutely or relative to other innovations in the history of humanity? Could a tetradic social structure develop without the use of language (logically, sections could be identified by contrasted body markings as effectively as by names, and egocentric categories by contrasted styles of behaviour as effectively as by kinship terms)? Can one argue that a division into absolutely identified groups preceded one into relatively identified categories, that (to put it crudely) the egocentric derives from the sociocentric? Were the rules structuring gatherings the first social rules? Might initiation have been the first ritual?

What I have been trying to do is (as in Chapters 2 and 3 above) to show the continuing usefulness of *Année sociologique* ideas for thinking about current problems.[10] If I am right, *Elementary Forms*, together with Mauss's essay on the Eskimos, helps to fill out tetradic theory and make it more relevant to palaeoanthropology. In any case, I think Durkheim draws attention to matters that cannot be neglected by those who think seriously about the origins of society.

Notes

1. The expression 'child-exchange' can also be applied to the quite different situation where, for instance, some members of patriclan or patrimoiety A exchange children on a temporary or permanent basis with patriclan or patrimoiety B. If all members of A gave their children to B, children would cease to belong to their father's group and the 'patri-' would become meaningless.

2. The preceding discussion does little more than rephrase the insights of Granet, who was well aware of the significance of *double bipartition* (1939: 170–71) in the simplest forms of social organisation. In the understanding of elementary structures of kinship Granet's priority relative to Lévi-Strauss has been well analysed by Héran (1998).

3. In connection with the world-historical approach to gender studies one notes that, at this level of abstraction, sections and social classes in the modern sense have in common that ego's place in society depends equally on both parents, while in social structures based on unilineal descent one parent is more significant than the other.

4. In his lectures for 1910/11 Mauss claimed to have 'established the unity of initiation cults and totemic cults, and tried to reconstruct the ritual that had served as the common origin of both' (II: 259).

5. It is a pity too that Durkheim could not or did not draw on the critical observations by Mauss, made in his thesis (09, I: notes 160, 281), on the ethnography of Spencer and Gillen.

6. See Lourandos (1988: 150), who argues, with reference to Australia, that 'the context for change' was provided by 'the arena of intergroup relations (for example, feasting, ritual and exchange)'. Although as an analyst I used the notion of a bounded totality in constructing the tetradic model, and although I assume that the original inventors did likewise, it does not follow that in reality social boundaries were impermeable.

7. See Quiatt and Reynolds, who rightly see tetradic theory as a challenge to their

ideas, in that it is difficult to reconcile with any simple notion of continuity from primate to human patrilineages (1993: 286).

8. In 1904 Hubert and Mauss thought that the only instinct a sociologist could recognise was that of sociability (*SA*: 120), but I cannot be sure how relevant this is.

9. Not to mention Granet (1939: 175–77), who writes of the rhythm of social life and frequently draws on dance in his references to the *chassé-croisé* of domestic life. See also McNeill (1995), a reference I owe to Andrew Sherratt.

10. Cf. Prades (1987: 142): 'The essential interest of Durkheimian thought consists in its power to stimulate us'.

Chapter 5

MAUSS AND THE CATEGORIES

Every reader of Mauss knows that his work is scattered, heterogeneous, and difficult to pin down, that it resists simplifying formulae
and is suggestive rather than systematic. He himself sometimes dis-
couraged a search for its unifying principles, telling an American
interviewer in the 1930s: 'I am not interested in developing systematic
theories' (Murray 1989: 165). People have even spoken of his 'dread
of system-building', his *horreur de l'esprit de système* (Caillé 1996:
184).

Nevertheless, his œuvre represents the effort of a single mind, and
one should not so easily give up the attempt to find within it some sort
of intellectual unity. As Steven Lukes put it (1996: 44), in a comment
on Fournier's biography of Mauss, this is a search that historians of
the human sciences can hardly duck. And it is even more incumbent
on those of us in whom Mauss inspires not only dispassionate scientific
appreciation but also a feeling of warmth or affection. In any case,
whatever motivates investigators, the search continues. For instance,
people ask whether the foundation or the core of Mauss's contribution
is to be found in his idea of the total social fact or the total human
being, in his notion of the gift, or in his belief that *mana* was more fundamental than Durkheim's sacred (Berthoud and Busino 1996).

Categories in general

Without at all denying the interest of these ideas, I should like to suggest another approach to the problem of the coherence of Mauss's
thought, by focusing on the notion of categories. This is of course a
major theme in Durkheim, but it is also widely present in the work of
Mauss. It appears already in 1903 in his joint essay with Durkheim on
primitive classification, and it is still there when he discusses the

notion of matter in 1939 (II: 13–89, 161–68). From between these dates one might mention the oft-cited text of 1924 (*SA*: 309), which Lévi-Strauss placed so prominently at the end of his introduction to the first volume that assembled a set of Mauss's essays: 'We need to draw up the largest possible catalogue of categories... We shall see then that there are still plenty of moons – dead, pale or obscure – in the firmament of reason' (1950: li–lii). Even so, it seems that little effort has so far been made to gauge the significance of the notion of categories for anyone who aspires to grasp the coherence of this dazzling but disconcerting body of work.

Let me start with two clarifications. The first is a point of method. For the present purpose there is no need to limit oneself to what Mauss says explicitly. For one thing, Mauss sometimes keeps things back. In the 1924 paper, which was given to the Société de Psychologie, when one of the discussants brought up the problem of categories, Mauss explained that he had not ventured to broach it since 'we still need numerous preliminary studies [*travaux d'approche*]. Undoubtedly, it is quite premature to give anything more than pointers' (*SA*: 309). In any case, even if one wants to, no one succeeds in giving a perfect and exhaustive expression to their own ideas, and certainly Mauss did not. For example, when reading his intellectual self-portrait of 1930 (Mauss 1996; 1998), one might conclude that the study of categories really only concerned that part of his work that dealt with 'Institutions'; but as we shall see, this is far from clear.

My second clarification bears on whether categories are a philosophical notion or an ethnographic one.[1] Of course, the word itself comes from philosophical discourse, and the idea of a list of categories has a long history within that discipline (Aristotle, Kant, Renouvier, Peirce, etc.). When using the word, Durkheim essentially wanted to rethink the categories from a sociological point of view, but in doing so he, and Mauss even more so, modified the notion. Let us take Mauss. From time to time he referred to the Aristotelian list, for instance when – at the age of 66 – he presented to British colleagues his 'sample of the work of the French school of sociology' (i.e., *The Person* – see Chapter 1, this volume). But he did not limit himself to that list. In the 1924 text cited above he goes on to say: 'The Aristotelian categories are in fact not the only ones that exist in our minds, or that have existed in the human mind', and as examples of other categories he gives the small and the great, the animate and the inanimate, right and left. In thus enlarging the Aristotelian list, he was drawing (as I showed in Chapter 1) not only on ethnography but also on linguistics.

However, the passage from the philosophical sense of category to the ethnographic and linguistic sense introduces ambiguities that Collins (1985) identifies clearly. From the philosophical point of view the categories are 'almost inseparable from the normal functioning of the mind'; they are like 'the skeleton of our understanding', says Durkheim (*EF*: 13). Since they are necessarily universal, they must stand outside cultural variation – they are etic. But if one follows Mauss and envisages categories as moons subject to death and (one assumes) birth, they cease to be universal and enter the emic domain of intercultural variability.

Although he does not expatiate on it, I think that Mauss was aware of the ambiguity: 'Our music is only *one* music. And yet, there exists something that merits the name simply of "music". That something is not our "musical grammar", but the latter is part of it. It is the same with all the great groupings of social phenomena' (34, II: 152) – and he goes on to mention science, technology, mysticism, poetry, and also systems of law and morality, grammars and logics. Thus he simultaneously recognises a universal, pan-human substratum (*un fond commun*) and the forms taken by this substratum in a particular society. This is the point on which Collins criticises Mauss's treatment of the category of the person, denying apparently that the category is universal, or at least, necessarily so.[2] But is it really possible to conceive of a system of law and morality that completely does without even an implicit notion of the human person who lives the system? Mauss's vocabulary is ambiguous, but I doubt if he was as confused as Collins thinks.

One might also wonder how helpful it is to draw too sharp a distinction between categories deriving from the philosophical tradition and those deriving from ethnographic or linguistic analysis. From the sociological viewpoint that Mauss would have taken, the tradition of Western philosophers is just as susceptible to sociological understanding as any other tradition, for instance, that of Indian philosophy. This is essentially the point made by Benveniste (1966: 63ff.), when he connects the Aristotelian list with the structure of the Greek language and imagines how different the list would be if it had been produced by a speaker of the Ewe language in Togo.

Let us now move to the central question, which is the importance of categories, philosophical or otherwise, for a global conceptualisation of the contribution of Mauss. In general, to understand the relation between A and B, one needs to understand both of them. An answer to the present question would therefore require not only a knowledge of Mauss's work, but also an understanding of an issue that is deeply embedded in the whole history of philosophy. Moreover, to acquire this understanding would not be easy, since philosophers disagree both over the list of categories and over the very meaning of the word. Aristotle's list is 'perhaps the most heavily discussed' of all the notions of that thinker, according to Smith (1995: 55; cf. Frede 1987: 29–48);

'in philosophy the notion of category is notoriously and perhaps irremediably obscure' (Michel Bourdeau, according to Quéré 1994: 9). I cannot hope to dissipate the obscurities recognised by professionals, and if I nonetheless persist in posing the question it is because it is so important for understanding Mauss.

To arrive at a preliminary idea of what the categories meant to Mauss one needs to bring together several different sources, starting, of course, with what he himself says about them. However, Mauss presents himself as the associate and continuator of Durkheim, and what Durkheim says also needs to be taken into account. Indeed, one must go further and draw into the picture those philosophers who most influenced Durkheim, possibly Octave Hamelin, the disciple of Renouvier, and certainly Renouvier himself. The profound influence of Renouvier on French liberal republicans towards the end of the nineteenth century was noted by Lukes, who also quotes Durkheim's own remark that 'my educator was Renouvier' (1973: 54). Lukes offers a substantial list of the features in Renouvier that Durkheim might have appreciated, for instance, his critique of the Kantian doctrine of the *a priori* character of the categories. But one should also emphasise the importance of the very notion of category.

> A system of categories that was complete, luminous, so well articulated that its own ordering would appear to constitute its proof . . . would constitute a perfected philosophy. This science of sciences would have as its true name 'general logic'. (cited by Anon. 1867: 575)

The aim of the Durkheimian School was of course to construct a perfected sociology rather than a perfected philosophy, but even so, one can glimpse a continuity between the ambition Renouvier proposed for philosophy and the ambition that Mauss proposed for sociology. I am thinking again of Mauss's dream of a 'catalogue of all the categories which we can know that humanity has employed' (*SA*: 309).

Particular categories

Let us move now to the individual categories, starting in the natural place, with the list of Aristotle. It is a rather curious list, without any obvious system. It consists of ten items, though one also finds shortened forms with eight or six items, or even fewer. The full list appears twice (*Categories* 4, *Topics* 1.9), in the same order both times: substance (or essence), quantity, quality, relation, space, time; then position (or posture), possession (or condition), activity, passivity.

The first six are expressed in Greek by means of interrogative expressions – substance by *ti esti* 'what is?', quantity by *poson* 'how much or how many?', etc. – while the last four are expressed by infinitive forms of verbs.

Mauss makes virtually no allusion to the last four categories, and at first sight, in spite of the reference to Aristotle, he might seem only to have studied three out of the first six, namely substance, space and time. He planned to bring together manuscripts left by Hubert at his death as well as work of his own so as to publish a substantial exploration of the category of substance (1996: 234); he and his pupil Czarnowski had studied the category of space;[3] and Mauss had had an input into Hubert's essay on time. But if one reads Aristotle's list in the light of Renouvier, it becomes clear that the Durkheimian team had studied at least two others out of the first six. Renouvier, who omits substance, recognises the following nine categories: relation, number, position, succession, quality; then becoming, causality, finality, personality.

In contrast to Aristotle, Renouvier presents his list as a system (Anon. 1867; Hamelin 1927). The nine items form a well-ordered series: after relation, which is the basis of the system, there are two groups of four, the first associated with stability, the second with activity. The list progresses from the simple to the composite, from the abstract to the concrete, from what is far from consciousness to what is close to it. Furthermore, Renouvier takes from Kant the idea of associating each category with three other abstractions, presented under the headings thesis, antithesis, synthesis. So his category of quality is associated with 'difference, class [*genre*], species', that of number with 'unity, plurality and totality'.

So when Mauss talks of the category of *genre* which he had studied with his uncle in 1903, he no doubt had in mind the Aristotelian category of quality (Greek *poion* 'what sort of?'); and when he presents Durkheim's *Elementary Forms* as having studied the category of totality (27, III: 185), he was surely thinking of Aristotle's quantity. If so, the Durkheimian school in general and Mauss in particular were interested in five of the six categories of Aristotle. Only one is missing, the fourth, that of relation (Greek *pros ti* 'towards or against what?').

If we look at Renouvier's list the picture is somewhat similar. All the categories in the first set of four interested Mauss, for Renouvier's number, position, succession, quality correspond to Mauss's totality, space, time, class; and from the second set of four, causality and personality correspond to Mauss's cause and person (he discussed cause in his 1904 essay on magic and *mana*). But what about relation? As already noted, Renouvier regarded relation as the first foundation (*la base première*) of the whole system. It was the 'category of categories' (Hamelin 1927:102), and in a certain sense was shared by all the others. Thus it is out of the question that Durkheim and Mauss could have been unaware of this fundamental doctrine of Renouvier. Although Mauss never puts this category in parallel with others studied by Durkheimians, indeed, never even alludes to it as a category, it seems obvious that he must have reflected on it sociologically.

The category of relation

In fact Mauss did more than reflect on the category. In spite of his surprising silence, I think that he studied it at some length in several of his texts, including some of his most celebrated. I can only account for his silence by supposing that he regarded these texts as no more than 'preliminary approaches', and for that reason judged it premature to use the philosophical terminology to indicate the orientation of his work.

So which are these texts? Roughly speaking, they are those to which he alludes under the heading of 'Institutions' in the self-portrait of 1930, which relate to social relations rather than to 'Religion and Ideation'. The former title covers the following:

1. the review of Steinmetz;
2. the essays on Eskimos, on polysegmentary societies, and on joking relationships;
3. the texts on reincarnation and the inheritance of the name (*prénom*) within the clan;
4. above all, of course, *The Gift*.

One might be misled by the title of the last text, if it were taken simply as implying the interpretation of objects. The word 'gift' implies the verb give, and verbs in general are either one-place (A comes), or two-place (A strikes B), or three-place (A gives B to C). So the gift B is related both to the giver A and the recipient C. But in spite of such complications, what matters is the relation between the giver and recipient that is established via the gift – as becomes obvious when the prestation is not a material object but a service (A serves B). In any case, Mauss himself says (ibid.) that what he had wanted to study was reciprocities, antagonisms and rivalries. Moreover, although *The Gift* focuses on agonistic exchange, this is presented as merely a development of the system of total prestations; and the purest type of the latter – for Mauss – consisted in the alliance of two exogamous moieties in Australian or North American tribes, where 'everything is complementary and takes for granted the collaboration of the two halves of the tribe' (25, *SA*: 151, 227). Reciprocity, alliance, collaboration – such words show that fundamentally the essay is about social relations. This is not new (cf. Godelier 1996: 142), indeed it is probably obvious. But I am proposing that we read *The Gift*, not simply as a study of social relations, but as a preliminary study bearing on the category of relation.

Let us go a little further. The importance of the notion of relation in structuralism is well known, as is Lévi-Strauss's debt to Mauss in his *Elementary structures of kinship*. The alliance theory of structuralist anthropologists essentially derives from the Maussian concept of the exchange of women. Such exchange however, is normally intragenerational or horizontal, while kinship also involves the equally important intergenerational or vertical dimension. Mauss was enormously interested in the latter, for instance when he talked about the transmission of the name and the soul between alternate generations, and as I have shown above in Chapter 3, he even began to think about this dimension in terms of exchange.

The point is that the major possibilities for the bisection of a society are not simply exogamous patrimoieties and exogamous matrimoieties: a society can also be bisected (both logically and in real life) into endogamous generation moieties. In the latter case the relation between the moieties is not the exchange of women but the exchange of children. We, the members of moiety A, received the gift of life from our parents in moiety B, and we return the gift in the form of our children, who will also belong to moiety B, and will ensure its continuance into the future. At the level of events (as distinct from formal models), one can imagine the exchange taking place not at birth but at initiation (Allen 1998a: 159; Chapter 4, this volume). Here, as in Maori law, but in an even stronger sense, 'to present something to someone is to present something of oneself' (*SA*: 161); one's child is one's property in a sense that is very special and perhaps prototypical. This is not the place to elaborate the point, but I would like to suggest (as indeed have many others) that even today we have not exhausted what Mauss can teach us about gifts.

Let us move from kinship to an even larger question. It was particularly in the context of gifts that Mauss spoke of his famous 'total facts', those that 'put in motion the whole collectivity, economic, moral and religious, aesthetic and mythic'.[4] Thus although *The Gift* once presents itself (*SA*: 266) as a response to the question posed by Durkheim (*EF*: 598 n.2) concerning the notion of economic value, its true theme goes far beyond the domain of economics. In fact, the exchange relations that it discusses pervade all social life. But does not this insight echo Renouvier's view that the category of relation penetrates all the other categories? This omnipresence of social relations is expressed in another way in his *Self-portrait* when Mauss writes: 'Part of the method consists precisely in connecting the facts of institution and structure to the facts of mentality, and conversely' (1996: 231).

Concluding questions

There is still a lot to be said about Mauss and categories, and I can only offer here a few disconnected comments.

I have tried in Chapter 2 to develop Mauss's ideas on the category of class by connecting them with the theoretical approach of Dumézil. I believe that, via Granet, Dumézil greatly profited from the essay of Durkheim and Mauss, and that the functional ideology of the Indo-Europeans is an example of a primitive form of classification; but I also believe that the triadic framework within which Dumézil envisaged the ideology is too narrow (Allen 1996a). This will all need more work, but one narrower question is whether Mauss would have thought that for the early Indo-Europeans, a function (say the second function, which pertains to physical force and war) was itself a category.[5]

On the category of substance, as I mentioned, Mauss hoped to publish in posthumous collaboration with Hubert a major work in two or three volumes. How far can one go in reconstructing and developing Mauss's ideas on this category (see Allen 1998e)?

One might wonder whether Mauss reflected on the four final categories of Aristotle, the first of which is position or posture (Greek *keisthai*), for example, being seated or lying. Might this category lurk somewhere in the background to Mauss's essay on the techniques of the body?

How did Mauss envisage (or how could he have envisaged?) the relations between the categories? One knows that he had reservations about the approach of Lévy-Bruhl, who tried in one leap to grasp primitive mentality as a concept, without dividing it into categories (Chapter 1, this volume), and also that he touched on the question in his analysis of *mana*. *Mana* was 'successively and simultaneously quality, substance and activity' (04, *SA*: 102 – note the final word); it was a special category of primitive thought and the first form of the categories of substance and cause (08, I: 29). Would it be possible to systematise these remarks?

Similarly, what is to be said about the idea of using Aristotle's list as a convenient mode of division of labour among the members of the Durkheimian team?

Mauss was of course an evolutionist in the sense that he looked at social phenomena in the context of global history, and I suggested in 1985 that for him the process that had dominated the world history of each category was one of homogenisation (in other words, just the opposite of the process of differentiation that some evolutionists would envisage). For example, whereas for many tribal societies each region of space has its own value, for modern science space is a continuum lacking such qualitative differentiation. So can one interpret monetisation from the same point of view? Does not the general trend from systems based on gifts to systems based on the market represent a process of homogenisation of social relations?

Lots of questions posed, few answers given. Nevertheless, I hope to have shown that Aristotle's categories offer an approach to understanding not only the orientation of the Durkheimian enterprise in general but also the personal thinking of that member of the school who, at least to some of us, is the most interesting and inspiring of them all.

Notes

1. I should like to acknowledge here my debt to Collins 1985 (which has recently appeared in French translation), and also to the tutorial teaching of Rodney Needham who, in 1965, proposed to me 'the study of categories' as a definition of the discipline on which I was just embarking.
2. Collins may be thinking of Buddhism, on which he is a specialist.
3. On Czarnowski see Isambert (1983), Sadowska (1986) and Anon. (1940). This last, which is an interesting obituary, is signed *Les Annales sociologiques*, but should probably be included in the bibliography of Mauss.
4. On the occasion of the Mauss colloquium in Paris in 1997, Denise Paulme recalled that Mauss liked Wagner – a reminiscence that is also recorded by Fournier (1994: 616). Has anyone explored the relation between the total social fact and the *Gesamtkunstwerk*?
5. Although one might regard it as an example of a category in the ethnographic sense, it is probably better to see the second function as one of the forms taken, over a certain stretch of cultural space-time, by the more abstract and fundamental notion of class. One needs to think of categories as existing on different levels of abstraction (cf. Schmaus 1998).

Chapter 6

REFLECTIONS ON MAUSS AND CLASSIFICATION

Techniques of the Body, probably Mauss's best known text after *The Gift*, began life in 1934 as a lecture to the Société de Psychologie in Paris, yet it is only intermittently and towards the end that its bearing on psychology is raised explicitly. The initial presentation points elsewhere (*SA*: 365ff.). Having helped to found the Institut d'Ethnologie ten years previously, Mauss had been giving an annual course of lectures there, and he introduces his 1934 paper as answering a problem he had encountered in organising the course. Though long aware of cultural differences in the use of the body, he had previously not seen how to categorise them except under the unsatisfactory label of 'miscella-neous' (*Divers*). He now saw that they fell under the label 'technology'.

When he originally labelled these ethnographic facts as *Divers*, Mauss was presumably conscious of the classification of book reviews in the *AS*. From volume 2 onwards the journal had used the following seven first-order sections or rubrics (themselves subdivided). First came a series of types of sociology: I general, II religious, III moral and juridical, IV criminal, V economic; then, heterogeneously, VI social morphology and VII *Divers*. Rubric VII had come to cover the sub-headings of aesthetics, linguistics and technology, though *Divers* had also been used as a subheading within other major rubrics.

To Mauss and his uncle these headings were important (cf. Favre 1983). From a practical viewpoint, different rubrics had different edi-tors, so they bore on the division of labour among the *équipe* working for the journal; but there was more to it. The aim of the journal was to cover the whole field of sociology – that is, of *faits sociaux* as defined by Durkheim in the *Rules of Sociological Method*, or by Fauconnet and Mauss in their encyclopaedia article of 1901 (III: 139ff.). Like any other science, sociology had to classify and arrange the facts that it dis-covered. Looking back on the *AS* in 1930 Mauss wrote: 'Above all we attempted, and myself particularly, to incorporate the facts within social theory [*doctrine*] and simultaneously to organise them'; and the schema they established had been followed by other writers (1998: 36). Thus the rubrics represented a classification, not merely of the literature, but of social phenomena.

It is this broader ambition that lies behind the 1934 paper. If Mauss is so pleased at rescuing phenomena such as styles of swimming from the ragbag heading of *Divers*, it is because, while not wishing to exaggerate the significance of such taxonomic exercises, he valued the substitution of order for disorder in our ideas (*SA*: 372). And as if to emphasise even more clearly his interest in classification, the paper goes on explicitly to offer two alternative ways of classifying the techniques of the body. Here, as often, we encounter Mauss the Lover of Classifications, or in brief, Mauss the Classifier.

Since classification is such a pervasive theme in Mauss's œuvre, I cannot hope to be systematic. However, in spite of the increasing attention being given to his thought (James and Allen 1998; Karsenti 1997), there is still so much to do that even unsystematic reflections may be useful. In any case, my interest lies not only in studying one of the 'greats' of twentieth-century social thought, but also, and more so, in trying to develop his ideas by turning them in new directions – one of which will eventually lead us back to the body. I start by noting four different senses in which Mauss was interested in classification.

Four modalities of classification in Mauss

1. The AS classification of social facts

Already in 1901 the encyclopaedia article ends with a section on the divisions of sociology. 'Sociology adopts and makes its own the great divisions already observed by the various sciences that compare institutions – comparative law, religion or political economy – sciences of which sociology claims to be the successor' (III: 175). But while appropriating what is useful in the results of the older 'special sociologies', it bridges the divides between them and thereby transforms them. A quarter-century later Mauss is still thinking hard about these issues: in 1927, commenting on the new postwar series of the *AS*, he devotes a whole article to 'Divisions and proportions of divisions in sociology'. The article starts apologetically. The new series has retained the framework of the old, the *cadre* that Durkheim gradually elaborated, but this is due to the inertia of tradition and to lack of time; it is not because the old framework is theoretically ideal (III: 178). I return later to the content and ordering of the old rubrics.

2. The 'biological' classification

Having noted the defects of the *AS* classification, Mauss develops Durkheim's alternative proposal (in *The Rules*) that the primary division of sociological phenomena should be into morphological and physiological. Both alternatives have uses (just as in 1934 both classifications of body techniques are presented as worthwhile), but the 'biological' is less ethnocentric, less abstract and clearer (III: 204). I put 'biological' in quotes because, while retaining Durkheim's vocabulary, Mauss recommends dissociating the labels from their biological connotations (III: 206). In this binary schema, social morphology remains, as in *AS* rubric VI, the study of the group 'qua material phenomenon'. The materiality of society consists in countable situated human beings living, moving and working in time and geographical space, and it will form the solid basis of the sociology to which we should aspire (III: 208, cf. *M*: 15).[1] As an example, Mauss refers to his 1906 essay on the contrasting summer and winter demography of the Eskimos (*SA*: 389ff.), which was subtitled 'a study in social morphology'. As for social physiology (an expression that goes back to Saint-Simon), it covers on the one hand behaviour and institutions, on the other, ideas and representations, though these two facets are as intimately linked as body and mind in psychology. In this way it embraces all that remains of the social – everything non-morphological, including the old special sociologies (primarily religion, law and economics). These subject areas can continue to develop, but as parts of the embracing discipline of sociology itself. The *completeness* of the latter arises because 'in a collectivity there are evidently only three groups of collective phenomena: the mass of individuals, their acts and their ideas' (III: 212).

3. Categories

To judge from a considerable number of scattered references, this must have been one of Mauss's favourite topics for reflection (Chapter 5, this volume). If categories are simply 'the most fundamental divisions of some subject matter' (Lacey 1995), the matter in question here is human thought; indeed Mauss sometimes refers to the categories under the heading of 'the problem of reason' (08, I: 26; 1996: 234). According to Durkheim's classic discussion (*EF*: 13), these essential notions can be thought of as the solid frames that embrace thought (*les cadres solides qui enserrent la pensée*) or as the bony skeleton of the understanding (*l'ossature de l'entendement*). For Mauss, as for his uncle, the word primarily connoted the ten-item list of Aristotle, the starting point for the lists of later Western philosophers, but Mauss was quick to add that the Western lists are not exhaustive. Other cultures have other categories.

Mauss tends to present the categories more as a list than as a classification (e.g., *M*: 247). A well-known passage recommends that the
discipline draw up a maximally full 'catalogue' of categories (*SA*: 309),
which should start by embracing all those that we can know humanity to have used. The implication is both that some are lost in the
undocumented past and that new ones may emerge in the unforesee-
able future. It may be partly the lack of a well-defined totality that here
deters Mauss from talking of a classification, but whatever his reasons,
a catalogue of categories would surely constitute a classification of
humanity's fundamental ideas.

Furthermore, from a different point of view, just as the *AS* classification of social facts facilitated the division of labour among the section editors and reviewers, so the categories served to distribute tasks
among the researchers, the writers of the memoirs that at first preceded the reviews. Each researcher could focus on one or more categories. Thus Hubert took time, Czarnowski space, Mauss himself the
person, substance and also, I think (Chapter 5 above), relation. The
pattern was set by Durkheim and Mauss writing in 1903 on the category of quality or class (Chapter 2, this volume).

How did the categories relate to the *AS* classification of social facts?
For Durkheim the answer was pretty clear: the principal categories at
least were born in and from religion, were a product of religious
thought (*EF*: 13 again). Mauss disagreed. He was confident that they
belonged under general sociology. They were in fact the ultimate goal
of the whole discipline. They would crown our studies and synthesise
them (III: 185), and perhaps one day inspire the best philosophy (*SA*:
310). But since there was still so much to explore, he would have
thought it premature to use them as a basis for organising the journal.

4. Primitive classification

The French original of *PC* was entitled 'On certain primitive forms of
classification' (sometimes the text talks of types rather than forms, but
without clear difference of meaning), and it examined three main
forms – Australian, North American (mainly Zuñi) and Chinese – seen
as forming an evolutionary or world-historical sequence. However, the
authors are less than explicit on what makes these forms 'primitive'. It
cannot be the technology of the users, if only because of the literate
Chinese. The small number of hierarchical levels in the taxonomies
may be relevant, but is not the main point. The primitive quality lies
rather in the linking of classifications or lists belonging to one context
or domain with those belonging to another. A scientific world-view
admits no link between groupings of society, the division of the year
into seasons and lists of totemic animals, while it is just such links that
characterise the primitive equivalent.

To think about these issues one can first envisage each context or domain with its divisions or list laid out in a row, and then show the links by means of vertical alignment (as in Lévi-Strauss 1962: 56). In the simplest case the classification will then appear as a rectangular table of rows and columns, each cell containing one entry. The interesting questions here concern the nature of the columns.

A society that favours (say) triadic classifications allows one to construct a three-column table, each row having three entries. But this alone does not amount to a primitive form of classification. For that, the vertical alignments must be meaningful within the society, must in some sense themselves constitute classes. In the simplest case the native ideology would itself provide a label (perhaps a totem) covering all and only the items in a column, but there are other possibilities. For instance, the position of the column (left to right) might reflect rank (high to low), or some quality or feature other than rank might run through a column. Such a quality need not possess a label in the native language, nor need each entry be felt to participate in the column in the same way – overlapping partial linkages are enough. But whereas any classification implies at least a row (a list of categories covering a domain or context), it does not become a primitive one without the columns. The primitiveness is defined by the vertical or paradigmatic dimension.

The 1903 essay also discussed a 'third' dimension, the hierarchical one along which totalities are broken down into taxa of greater or lesser inclusiveness. But this sort of organisation applies to rows and not to columns, which are rarely and with difficulty conceptualised as articulated totalities. Moreover, such taxonomic hierarchy is not a *sine qua non* for primitive classifications, being often absent, for example, in the European mediaeval linkages of elements, humours, ages of man, colours, etc.

One of the best examples of a primitive form of classification was not discovered until close to the end of Mauss's active career. I refer to the Indo-European world, as analysed by Dumézil. In this case, the well-known three functions are (as it were – for Dumézil does not use the tabular model) the labels provided by the analyst for the columns resulting from the analysis. Pooling material taken from the various branches of Indo-European culture, especially from their earlier history, one can nowadays assemble many scores of rows. Can one be more precise? Since contexts often merge into each other, exact totals would be meaningless, but one might think in terms of three figures. However, what matters is the importance and variety of the contexts.

As Dumézil saw, his comparative method enables us to reconstruct the pattern dominating the ideology of the proto-Indo-European speakers, but we can now supplement his own formulations in two ways. Firstly, we can add that the pattern was precisely a primitive form of classification; and secondly (e.g., Allen 1999b), we must expand the trifunctional schema with two further columns. The triads are a reduction, due either to the analyst or to the society, of an original and fundamental pentadic pattern. In this particular case, much as with the Chinese considered by Durkheim and Mauss, the native ideology provides no obvious labels for the columns (might a proto-list of 'canonical' deities once have served the purpose?). However, the columns are both ranked and united internally by common qualities, as expressed in the analyst's definitions of the functions. As elsewhere, I use the following labels and definitions (abbreviated):

- F4+ heterogeneous and supreme, often transcendent
- F1 pertaining to the sacred
- F2 pertaining to the physical force and war
- F3 pertaining to fecundity, wealth and related ideas
- F4- heterogeneous and excluded or somehow devalued

The middle three are the familiar Dumézilian functions, their definitions modified only by removal of sovereignty from F1.[2]

The Indo-European case is relevant here, partly as basis for my later argument, partly as confirming the validity and distinctiveness of the phenomenon discussed by Durkheim and Mauss, and partly because I see its discovery as a development of Mauss's ideas (Chapter 2, this volume). As Dumézil often said, his insight into the three functions was an unexpected result of the teaching of Mauss's close friend, the Sinologist Granet, whose thinking was profoundly influenced by the 1903 paper.

In presenting these four modalities, we have, roughly speaking, moved from classifications produced by sociologists for their colleagues towards those produced by the people under study – from etic to emic.[3] The 'categories' occupy a somewhat uneasy intermediate position, but Mauss at least located them close to the second pole. Possibly the 'biological' classification should have been presented before the *AS* one since Mauss himself regarded it as the more scientific. But moving on from the group as a whole, let us now consider relations between individual modalities. In a set of four items there are six pairs and four triads, so I shall have to be selective.

Selected relations between the modalities

1. Primitive Classifications and Categories

Although the 1903 essay is primarily a study of classification, its last paragraph refers to 'other fundamental notions of the understanding', including time, space, cause and substance. This clearly foreshadows Mauss's later discussions, in which class or quality (*genre* and *qualité* – M: 248) is just one in the series of categories examined by the French school. Why it was the first to be treated is partly a specialist question for historians of the school, but it is also worth asking whether it *ought* to have been the first, whether it has some intrinsic priority over some or all of the others.

Let us consider the place of time and space in primitive classifications.[4] The year is classified into four seasons both in the Zuñi and Chinese cases, and the latter also includes 'cycles of years, days and hours'. Within the Indo-European world the successive reigns of the (more or less) mythical kings of early Rome offer a clear temporal manifestation of the pentadic classification (Allen 1996b), and one can easily find the four seasons in the speculative classifications of European mediaeval thinkers. However, time is often closely linked to space – usually to the cardinal points, with or without centre, zenith and nadir. Thus, in the Zuñi case the seven divisions of space actually provide labels for what we have been calling the columns (having arguably taken over this role from totemic species), and in 1934 when Granet devotes book II of *La pensée chinoise* to *les idées directrices*, he starts with a chapter on time and space. Stressing the qualitative heterogeneity attributed to divisions within each category, he adds that 'to each individualised portion of time corresponds one portion of space' (1968: 77). Centre and cardinal points correlate with representatives of the functions in various Indo-European contexts (e.g. Allen 1996a).

So time and space commonly contribute rows to primitive classifications. Space may take on an additional role as label, but as such it could be replaced by other labels or by none, and it is in no sense constitutive. To repeat, what defines these world-views is the cross-cutting of the horizontal and vertical dimensions, of internally differentiated domains with the particular qualities that run through a column. I doubt that Durkheim and Mauss had thought the matter through in 1903 but, seen in this light, the category of class *is* more fundamental than space or time. Mauss himself singled out this 'effort' as among the most philosophical that had been attempted by sociology (1998: 40), but did he fully appreciate its significance?

The question we have asked of time and space needs to be asked of other categories, in particular of substance and person, which are not unconnected. In fact, both the Zuñi and Chinese classifications incorporate elements (wind/air, water, fire, earth in the former), and the same list is prominent in European schemes of correspondences (perhaps as part of the Indo-European tradition, though the details are not clear). However, the elements are only one aspect of substance, and not the most salient one sociologically. Mauss was deeply interested in this category (Allen 1998e), and especially in the link between substance and subsistence or food – the source of our bodily substance.[5] Dietary rules may of course apply not only to whole societies, but also to sub-units such as clans. More precisely, they may apply only after initiation, when an individual becomes a full member of a totemic clan. Potentially then, the groups that make up social structure can be conceived locally as differing in substance. But lists of such groups occur in the tribal schemes in the 1903 essay, so this line of thought brings us back to social morphology and its place in Mauss's classifications.

2. AS and 'biological' classifications

For Mauss, 'nothing is simpler than to define social phenomena and nothing is more difficult than to define the various categories of social phenomena' (27, III: 219). The *AS* classification embodied too much abstraction and prejudice, followed too closely the narrow classifications imposed by the traditional sciences of economics, law, religion, etc.

> The very titles of the special sociologies correspond too closely to the division of labour in modern society, to the divisions between activities in our western societies – divisions that are more presentist [*plus actuelles*] and more ephemeral than one tends to think. They are deeply marked by our own time and our own subjectivity. They fit poorly with the life of societies that have divided their labour in other ways or with the life of societies which will one day divide it in ways different from ours. (III: 204)

Having proposed the 'biological' classification and discussed its advantages, Mauss then, in a rich passage (III: 219–225), indicates how it should set about dividing up social phenomena by taking social morphology as its starting point. Beneath acts and representations one must look for the groups who perform or think them. Mauss even proposes something very like the tables discussed above:

> The specialities [religious, juridical, economic, etc.] partition the great classes of facts as it were into vertically disposed stacks [*piles*]; on the other hand one can also divide these partitions as it were into horizontal slices [*tranches*], by degrees or layers of increasing or decreasing ideation, of greater or lesser materialisation, according as one moves further from or closer to pure representation or material structure in the true sense (III: 224)

No doubt he envisaged social morphology as forming a slice or row at the base of the stacks or columns, and the most abstract concepts as a row at the top (corresponding to the 'native labels' mentioned above).

It is this ascending scale that he follows in his lecture course, which starts with social morphology and leads via technology, aesthetics and economy[6] to law, morals and religion. General sociology, the 'crown' of the subject, though hinted at (*M*: 14), is not treated, perhaps because the end of the academic year cut short the lecture series.

3. Primitive classification and the classifications of social facts

The foundational position of social structure or morphology in the 'biological' classification is its main difference from the *AS* classification, and when he criticises the latter it is the first point that Mauss makes (III: 180). Nevertheless, this position was part of Durkheimian doctrine well before references occur to the food-substance link. For instance, it is explicit in Durkheim's 1895 classification of social types in Chapter IV of *The Rules*, and in 1903 the analysis of Australian material starts from the four-section system, which is taken as typical: 'All the members of the tribe are thus classified within definite groupings [*cadres*] . . . and the classification of things reproduces the classification of people' (II: 20).

During the course of social evolution, the synchronic links between social structure and speculative classifications tend to become less clear and eventually fade out (as had happened in the Chinese case). One might expect the Indo-European speakers to resemble the Chinese in this, but in fact they are more like the Zuñi: a pentadic social structure (king; priests, warriors, free producers; serfs and outsiders) expresses a division of labour already recognised by the proto-society. We need not try to decide whether recruitment to these roles was unilineal (exogamous clans) or bilateral (endogamous strata) or something else, nor to what extent such a model corresponded to practice at any particular time or place. The point is that this classification of society correlates with the patterning of many other ideological domains and belongs within the same form of primitive classification.

Though the link between social structure and the rest of the classification soon faded out in the ancient Greek and Roman world, it seems not only to have survived into feudal Europe but to have enjoyed a revival (Celtic and/or Germanic channels of transmission have been suggested). Certainly, the three estates – the clergy, nobility (originally the warrior nobility) and the *tiers état* of merchants and free farmers, the *oratores*, *bellatores* and *laboratores* (Dumézil 1982: 237, Duby 1978) – do fit the classical Dumézilian functions and have above them the king (transcendent) and below them inferiors or outsiders of various kinds.

This brings us back to Mauss's critique of the *AS* classification of social facts. Although the journal actually had the seven rubrics listed above, Mauss speaks as if – apart from 'miscellaneous', which was meaningless or insignificant (III: 178, 181) – it only had five: general sociology, the three special sociologies and social morphology. In other words, he quite reasonably conflates the two parts of moral and juridical sociology, the larger dealing with origins (as a note on the contents page states) and the smaller covering criminality and the contemporary functioning of moral/legal systems. The triad of special sociologies (religious, juridical and economic) is mentioned no less than six times in the 1927 essay.[7]

We have already seen that for Mauss the *AS* rubrics reflect the division of labour in Western society, but he did not explain how. We can now suggest an answer. Do not the five rubrics reflect the pentadic Indo-European ideology, mediated perhaps by the model of society current under the *ancien régime?* General sociology, crowning the subject, dealt with phenomena that concerned 'the totality of social life' (III: 303). But this is precisely the realm of the king (F4+), who symbolises the unity of society and transcends its internal divisions. Within the triad, religion corresponds to the clergy (F1), economics to the producers (F3), and only the juridical domain remains problematic. As for social morphology, whose emphatic materiality contrasts with the actions and ideas covered by social physiology, its very label separates it from the various sociologies. Moreover its rank is clear from Mauss's metaphors. If general sociology is or will be the crown of the science, social morphology, already the best constituted part of the discipline (207), is the base. Alternatively, one can recall dominant attitudes to matter versus mind in the history of Western thought, or more particularly in Comte's hierarchy of sciences. From either viewpoint, however important the rubric is for our understanding, social morphology is in some sense 'lower' than the others, and could qualify as F4-.

We need to be clear. The five *AS* rubrics in question are labels for classes of social facts: each class of facts is seen as a stack or column ranged below one rubric. In the *AS* (as is commonest in Indo-European contexts) the lowest-ranking entity – here social morphology – comes last (right-most) in the sequence of rubrics, while the 'biological' classification reverses the order. But in either case, a rubric, though in principle reflecting a division present in social reality, represents the highest level of abstraction in the analytic scheme. Social morphology is thus one entry in this top row. But social morphology also consists of facts on the ground, of people divided into groups, and in this sense it forms the bottom row of the table. Whether Mauss himself clearly saw this distinction, I am not sure. Probably the vertical arrangement was the more salient in his mind: already in 1906 he talked of establishing 'that hierarchy of concepts – well made and corresponding solely to the phenomena in question – whose establishment is the aim of *sociologie* as of the other sciences' (I: 42).

To return to the main argument, a pentadic structure should ideally be interpreted as manifesting the Indo-European functions only if all five elements fit the definitions of the functions, but the link between the juridical domain and the second function is clearly problematic. The full definition of the latter is 'physical, brute force, and the uses of force – principally but not exclusively in war' (Dumézil 1958: 19). Worse still, the juridical can sometimes be found in Dumézil's definitions of the first function, which includes 'the relations of men among themselves under the gaze and the guarantee of the gods (law [*droit*], administration)' (ibid.). This makes sense, if only because traditional societies so often connect law with knowledge of the sacred. Nevertheless, the gap between the second function and the *AS* rubric 'juridical' is less wide than it seems and can be reduced starting from either end.

Firstly, the juridical domain, which is extremely broad, includes under its various subheadings moral notions, social and political organisation and domestic organisation (much of what is now called kinship),[8] as well as civil or penal law. Within this domain, the heading that comes closest to the notion of physical force is political organisation, for politics connotes power. Durkheim's deliberate exclusion of politics from the rubrics proper is discussed at some length by Mauss in 1927 (also by Favre 1983), and is justified by Mauss on the grounds that politics as such is an art. A sociological science of this art is conceivable, but it should be 'pitilessly' eliminated from pure sociology (III: 232), and treated as an applied branch of the subject. Mauss felt so strongly about this that he planned to exclude his projected work on the nation from the series of publications that continued the memoirs included in the first ten volumes of the *AS* (1998: 42). As to where the political might fit in his overall classification of the subject, he wavered. As he recognised in 1927 (III: 237), the *AS* had sometimes in fact treated it as a pervasive feature of society belonging under general sociology, and this seems to be the main thrust of his argument. An alternative was to make it a special component of the sociology of action, which (if I understand him) would be a horizontal slice through the columnar rubrics of the 'biological' classification (III: 239). Later, however, in 1934 (III: 310), he hesitantly reverts to the Durkheimian position and again locates the study of political organisation and functioning under the heading of law (*droit*). Durkheim's justification had been that the state, the political organ (*organisme*) of society, the constitution and the establishment of a sovereign power are juridical and moral phenomena (III: 237). This formulation situates politics and power within the juridical. But since the juridical so often involves enforcement, could one not reverse the relation of inclusion so that the juridical falls within the political? Many a feudal lord used the courts to maintain his power.

Looking at the gap from the Indo-European end, one notes that the
full definition of the second function cited above covers the use of force
outside war, for instance by police or, more generally, by any agent of
the state. Moreover, although shorter definitions such as 'warrior
force' have worked well for many manifestations of the old ideology, for
others a broader one may be needed, covering concepts such as
dynamism, energy and initiative. In practice, Dumézil himself implicitly accepts this, for instance (1941: 257–61; 1968: 493–6), when he
analyses trifunctionally the three parts of the human soul recognised
by Plato in the *Republic* (427e–434d). These are: intelligence or reason; spirit; and passion or appetite (such as hunger and thirst). The
spirited component (*to thumoeides*) covers '(a) fighting spirit, (b) what
makes a man indignant at injury and a coward when he feels himself
in the wrong, (c) ambition and competitiveness' (Guthrie 1975: 476),
and only meaning (a) accords precisely with 'warrior force'.[9] However,
the analysis is persuasive. Plato links the three elements of the psyche
with the three classes in his ideal society, the spirited with the
guardians or auxiliaries – and the latter combine the roles of civil service, military and police, being 'charged with the execution and imple-
mentation, if necessary by force, of government decisions' (Lee 1955:
38). As Dumézil also saw (1971: 256 n.2), the pattern recurs in
schematic human geography (*Rep.* 435e–436a): the Thracians and
neighbours in the north are reputedly vigorous and high-spirited (*thu-
moeidēs* again), the Greeks, implicitly in the centre, are characterised
by intelligence, the Phoenicians and Egyptians to the South are lovers
of wealth (i.e., respectively F2,1,3). Though classicists seldom recognise the fact, throughout this passage Plato is using part of the old
Indo-European classification, and the spirited component relates to the
second function. In other words 'warrior force', although a useful
summary, is a narrow formulation of the function.

My suggestion then is that the gap between the *AS* juridical rubric
and the second function is less than it seems. On the one hand the
rubric already covers an aspect of politics, and this could be given
greater weight. On the other, the military use of second-functional
force can easily extend to the political use. Indeed, there is a recognised Hindu classification of knowledge in which this extension is
overt. *The Laws of Manu* (7.43) instructs the king to acquire three
branches of learning. These are (I adjust the order): philosophy and
knowledge of the soul – F1; the eternal science of politics and punish-
ment, *daṇḍanīti* (where *daṇḍa* means the rod, symbol of the king's right
to use force) – F2; and finally, trades and enterprises, learned from the
people – F3. I am not suggesting that this passage influenced the *AS*
classification, but rather that both in their own ways derive from the
Indo-European ideology.

Admittedly, the Greek and Indian classifications are triadic, while the *AS* rubrics are (for Mauss, and in essence) pentadic. This is no more problematic than when in the Zuñi case the schema as a whole correlates with the extended set of seven cardinal points, while the four seasons correlate only with the ordinary four. In any case, among the Indo-Europeans, a triad is often a substructure situated within a larger pentadic whole – much as the triad of special sociologies is situated between general sociology and social morphology. This brings me to my final section.

Body and society

We have argued that, as Mauss was perhaps not far from seeing, the *AS* classification of social facts reflects the Indo-European primitive classification and, ultimately, I-E social morphology. It is because of the foundational significance of social morphology that *PC* recommends talking of sociocentrism rather than anthropocentrism (II: 87). Nevertheless, society (the mesocosm) and man (the microcosm) are sometimes correlated, and this raises a topic that would certainly have interested Mauss the Classifier. In writing on the category of the person (*SA*: 333ff.) he explicitly limited himself to *droit et morale*, to the juridical rubric or column, in terms of the interpretation discussed above. But like space, time and substance, the person too can be seen as providing a row.

In Hindu tradition the native model of social structure consists of king plus the three twice-born estates or *varṇas*, then the ritually excluded serfs. I have argued elsewhere (Allen 1999b) that these five elements reflect the Indo-European ideology, but I now emphasise their myth of origin (*Rig Veda* 10.90.11–12). This very succinct passage derives the *varṇas* from the primal man Puruṣa.

11. When they divided the Man, into how many parts did they apportion him? What do they call his mouth, his two arms, his thighs and feet?
12. His mouth became the Brahman; his arms were made into the Warrior; his thighs the people; and from his feet the Serfs were born. (tr. Doniger O'Flaherty)

The starting point is the whole undivided body (F4+ because the whole transcends the parts), and it is followed by the four body parts in descending rank (F1 to F4-).[10] The myth does not spell out the appropriateness of the particular body part to each *varṇa*, but clearly the vertical position corresponds to the social rank. Moreover, the mouth corresponds to the priest's expertise in the oral tradition of the Vedas, and the arms to the body part most saliently involved in the warrior's special skills. Can one go further? Perhaps the thighs are a euphemism for the genitals, or replace a term relating to the abdomen (somewhat as French *cuisse* 'thigh' derives from Latin *coxa* 'hip'); and the feet might be seen as the porters or vehicles of the body.

In Plato, the link between body parts and units of the ideal society is differently presented, but not without similarities. One must consult not the *Republic*, but the dialogue that ostensibly continues it – the *Timaeus*, which discusses the Creation. If the *Republic* linked the philosopher kings, auxiliaries and farmer/craftsmen (let us say F1,2,3 respectively) with the cognitive, spirited and appetitive parts of the soul, the *Timaeus* links the psychic components to body parts. The head contains reason, the divine immortal part of the soul, and is separated by the neck from the thorax, which contains the spirited part – here described as *philonikon* 'victory-loving' (70a). This is the better half of the mortal soul, and it is separated by the diaphragm from the worse half, the vegetative soul, which is subject to appetites for food and drink, as if it were a manger (*phatnon*) for the feeding of the body (70de). In this case then, the body-society link is not a matter of origins but is made indirectly via the tripartite soul; and none of the body parts are identical with those in the Vedic myth. Head contrasts with mouth (or face), thorax with arms, upper abdomen with thighs. Nevertheless, the correlated hierarchy of body parts and social units is sufficient to suggest a common origin – as indeed has been proposed by (among others) Dumézil (1971: 352), who cites further evidence.

A four-functional viewpoint takes us further. Plato recognises only three parts to the soul, which therefore lacks a parallel for the Indian serfs; but he repeatedly connects the soul with the body. 'The whole, compounded of soul and body, is called a living being' (*Phaedrus* 246c, as *Tim.* 87e, etc.). But the body itself connotes mortality, as in the traditional wordplay linking *sōma* 'body' with *sēma* 'tomb' (*Gorgias* 493a), and when the gods gave it to us, it was as a servant to our most divine part, the head (*Tim.* 44d). So we meet again the characteristic pentad: living being as totality; trifunctional triad, in order of descending value; devalued material body, associated with death.

A similar picture emerges from the well-known image linking the soul to a horse-drawn chariot in the *Phaedrus* (246ab, 253c–255). The comparisons are as follows. The charioteer, in charge, corresponds to the reasoning soul; the right-hand horse, the noble and disciplined one, to the spirited soul; the left-hand one, ugly and undisciplined, to the appetitive soul. The chariot itself is not given an interpretation in this particular passage, but elsewhere Plato presents the body as the soul's vehicle and means of transport (*okhēma kai euporia*, *Tim.* 44e, 69c). Moreover, as the only inanimate object in the schema, the chariot is closer than anything else to the body/tomb (F4-).[11] More remotely, as vehicle, it also corresponds to the feet of Puruṣa.[12]

I cannot here trace the long history of the Platonic model of the human being in Western thought, but I suppose that it still influences our concepts of mind, and in particular our tendency to attach value to the intellectual or cognitive aspects of the person, rather than to the will or emotions.[13] Is not this tendency detectable in Mauss's own attitude to the categories?

Near the end of their essay Durkheim and Mauss claim that distant influences from primitive forms of classification are still detectable today, but they think that what has endured is merely the abstract framework (*cadre*) of all classification (II: 88). I have argued here that there is more to it, that the *content* of the Indo-European primitive classification marked their own thinking, as no doubt it marks ours. I have also argued that, whether or not they saw this, the first category they chose for detailed study was a good choice, in that it can encompass several of the others.

Notes

1. It seems debatable just how far the expression covers the *ideas* that relate to the grouping of human bodies – certainly, ideas are given a subordinate role.
2. The justification for postulating a split fourth function is considered in my other papers, e.g., Allen (1996b). The notion will seem less arbitrary and odd if the ideology is envisaged as forming not a line but a circle, in which 'extremes' meet.
3. The four modalities I selected are not exhaustive. Thus in 1920 Mauss attempted a fourfold classification of 'the political forms of social life' (III: 579).
4. As has often been noted, Durkheim, following Hamelin, disagreed with Kant, who excluded time and space from the categories. In 1904 Hubert and Mauss contrast them with *mana* (*SA*: 112).
5. There are also hints that, in some contexts, substance is to mind as female is to male. Note that substance, the more material item in the first pair, correlates with the lower valued sex.
6. 'Of all moral phenomena economic ones are those that remain most deeply rooted in matter' (*M*: 123).
7. In one of these passages (III: 201) Mauss laments that, with the rubrics as they stand, 'one might think that, like our neighbours in British Social Anthropology, we [of the *AS*] know only *homo religiosus, ethicus, oeconomicus.*'
8. Accordingly, as Mauss put it in 1927 (III: 185), *PC* had seen the origin of the notion of class as 'primarily juridical': its basis was the clans or sections, i.e., kinship phenomena. However, arguably, in spite of the politico-legal aspects of domestic life, considerable tracts of 'kinship', especially its formal aspects, might be better placed under social morphology.
9. Another example, even remoter from warrior force, can be found in the branch of Hindu philosophy called Sāṃkhya, where *rajas*, the second-functional component of the material cosmos, has been rendered 'energy stuff' (Allen 1998e: 185)
10. In *The Laws of Manu* (1.31) the dismemberment theme is omitted: the Lord simply creates the *varṇas* from his own body parts.

11. The Kaṭha Upanishad (3.3–4) has a five-element image, less clearly linked to the functions, which I take to be cognate. The self is the rider in the chariot, the intellect is the charioteer, the mind is the reins, the senses are the horses, and *the body is the chariot*. This image is not related to the *varṇas*.

12. The feet of course correspond to the serfs, who are said to be only born once (i.e., biologically), in contrast with the superior *varṇas*, who are 'twice-born' because of their ritual initiation. Does not this suggest that the serfs are conceived of symbolically as somehow less animate, more like the chariot?

13. Compare, for example, Lyon 1997, who however, does not address Mauss's work as a whole.

Chapter 7

MAGIC, RELIGION AND INDO-EUROPEAN IDEOLOGY

This final chapter continues to reflect on Mauss's interest in classification but concentrates more narrowly on magic and religion, and it
uses Indo-European comparativism in a different way. While not
excluding the possibility that Mauss was influenced by this particular
intellectual tradition, I am more concerned here with using Indo-
European material as a test-case for thinking about the classification of
religious phenomena. How well do Mauss's formulations fit the data
from this part of the world? Let us start with Hubert, Mauss's close
friend and collaborator.

Religious phenomena and their classification

In his brief autobiographical note written in 1915, Hubert (1979:
203) claimed that the study of categories of collective thought was a
direction of research pioneered by himself and Mauss (*cette étude . . .
est notre originalité*). Working together on sacrifice (1899), they had
elicited the idea of the sacred as a category of mental operations
implicit in religious phenomena: 'Thence I went to time, Mauss to
space'.[1] The next joint work by the two friends was the essay on magic
(1904), which in retrospect Mauss tended to present as a study of the
category of cause (e.g., 38, *SA*: 334).

This category-focused reading of the essay is not without justification. 'Magic does indeed look like a gigantic variation on the theme of
the principle of causality' (*SA*: 56).[2] However, the essay puts little
emphasis on causation regarded as one category among others, as one
item in a list. Its focus is rather on *mana* which, as an underlying category (*SA*: 111–2), bears to magic much the same relation as the sacred
does to religion. Indeed, in the introduction to the essay (which is

oddly relegated to an appendix in *SA* itself, but restored to its correct position in the English translation), the authors present their second collaboration as a continuation of the first, almost as complementary to it. As a first approximation one is tempted to write sacred : religion :: *mana* : magic (where a single colon is read as 'is to', a double one as 'as').

However this formulation is rather simple, and the whole area bristles with problems. Among them are the following.

To what extent are religion and magic separable? The contrast between the extremes is clear enough. Some rituals are solemn, public, obligatory and regular, while others are illicit, prohibited and punishable. In the former we see the pole of sacrifice (representing religion), in the latter the pole of malefice or sorcery (representing magic); but in between one finds a confused mass of facts that are not easily classified. However, in spite of this continuum, humanity in general has both felt and acted out the contrast (*SA*: 13–15). In other words, the religion-magic polarity is both an ideal type for the analyst and a folk model.[3]

How should we define religion and the sacred? A key quotation here comes from the third Hubert-Mauss text, the joint introduction to their *Mélanges d'histoire des religions* (1909 – but the introduction came out separately the previous year).

> Sacrifice is a means for the profane to communicate with the sacred via the mediation of a victim.
>
> So what is the sacred? Following Robertson Smith, we conceived of it [in 1899] in the form of what is separated, what is prohibited. It seemed obvious to us that when something is prohibited for a group this is not simply the result of the cumulative misgivings of individuals. Accordingly we said that sacred things are social things [I: 306]. However, we now go further. In our view what is conceived as sacred is everything that, for the group and its members, qualifies society. If the gods, each when their time comes, leave the temple and become profane, we see on the other hand things that are human, but social – the Nation (*la patrie*), Property, Labour, the human person – enter in their stead one after the other. (08, I: 16–17)[4]

At first then, they saw sacred things simply as things that society separates from the everyday world and treats as special, so that access to them is hedged around with restrictions; the individual is socialised into making this distinction. Their later view gives the sacred a more positive content, which consists (it seems) in sociality itself. Moreover, the sacred needed to be seen as affective as well as cognitive, and as 'the idea-force around which rites and myths have been able to organise themselves' (ibid.). In this formulation, as so often in the work of the *Année*, one glimpses an anticipation of the later structuralist notion of conceptual entities underlying and generating what is observed. But the fundamental point for the writers ('the most certain gain of our work on sacrifice') lurks in the somewhat enigmatic phrase 'what for the group qualifies society'. They gloss this as meaning the 'identity of the sacred and the social'. No doubt a fuller gloss would refer to the Durkheimian view of society as a totality transcending the individual and constituting a *sui generis* level of reality.

How should we define magic and mana? The 1904 essay includes near its beginning a preliminary definition of magical rites as ones 'which are not part of an organised cult', which are 'private, secret, mysterious and in the limit tend towards being prohibited' (*SA*: 16). But these rites, like any others, derive from underlying representations, and in particular from the idea of *mana* (*SA*: 100–105). Meaning something like 'magical potency', this Melanesian and Polynesian word expressed an idea that Mauss took to be more or less universal, even if in other cultures it was sometimes covered by several different words or, not being clearly lexicalised, was left implicit. The idea straddles conceptual boundaries to which Europeans are accustomed, being at the same time a quality of agents or things, a substance or thing in itself, and an activity, power or force, often – but not always – mediated by spirits. Above all perhaps, it is a force, and one that tends to operate in a special milieu, a context or environment of its own. This marvellous or spiritual world is superadded to our everyday world of the senses and yet pervades it; it is both heterogeneous and immanent – as if it were a fourth dimension of space.[5]

What is the relation between mana *and the sacred, magic and religion?* Of the two underlying concepts, *mana* was the more general: one could probably say that if the sacred is the species, *mana* is the genus (*SA*: 112). In 1930 Mauss explicitly contrasted their 1904 view of *mana* with that of Durkheim, who later (i.e., in *EF*) 'tried to deduce it sociologically from the notion of the sacred' (1996: 234). In his *Manuel* Mauss reaffirms the greater generality of *mana* as follows.

> Just as aesthetics is defined by the notion of the beautiful, technology by technical effectiveness, just as economics is defined by the notion of value, law by the notion of property, *religious or magico-religious phenomena are defined by the notion of the sacred.* In the set of forces that are called mystical – we shall say *mana* – there are some that are *mana* to such a degree that they are sacred; these forces constitute religion in the strict sense, in contrast to the others which form religion in the broad sense. (*M*: 207–8)

Hubert and Mauss had planned to follow up their study of magic with a full treatment of the relation between magic and religion (*SA*: 140, 130; 08, I: 22). Mauss lectured on the subject in 1903/04, comparing the aims of magic and religion in Australia, Melanesia, North

America (Iroquois and Algonquins), Malaya, Vedic India, and ancient and mediaeval Europe (II: 390). Presumably it was in connection with this course that, with or without Hubert, he wrote a manuscript arguing that the relation between religion and magic was juridical – i.e., a matter of law, custom and morals – rather than logical – a matter of types of mental operation; and also that the relation varied between religions and societies (1996: 234). Unfortunately, in spite of Mauss's stated intention in 1930, the draft was never published and is no doubt lost for ever. Thus a student curious about Mauss's views on magic and religion has to make the best of the scattered statements that survive, at the same time taking due account of the complications that arise from changes in Mauss's own thinking. Following are two examples.

(1) Both in the essays on sacrifice (99, I: 199) and on magic (*SA*: 140), Hubert and Mauss explicitly disclaim macrohistorical concerns, but they were inevitably interested in them. They originally thought, for instance, that 'sacrifice was only practised where totemism does not exist or no longer exists', but later evidence from the Zuñi showed that the two forms of religion were not absolutely incompatible (08, I: 5–11, cf. 99, I: 197); and another instance of totemic sacrifice came to light among the Marind Anim of New Guinea (*M*: 220).

(2) In 1933, reacting to a paper by Granet on right and left in China, Mauss talks of changes in his views since the first decade of the century, when Hertz had written on right and left on the basis of Maori ethnography. Notions of taboo and correlations such as right : sacred :: left : profane were too absolute, took too little account of relativities in their application (what is right or left depends on which way you are facing). Moreover, when more emphasis is put on myth and representations, and less on ritual behaviour, the limitations of binary approaches to space become apparent even in the treatment of Maori material. In Hertz's time the notion of religion had been extremely restricted, being confined to the notion of the sacred, but for many purposes one needed much richer models, such as the sevenfold complex of cardinal points, zenith, nadir and centre (II: 143–8).

However, the student faces other sorts of difficulty too. Given the degree of collaboration among the central *Année* figures, one can hardly avoid relating Mauss's views to those of Durkheim and Hubert. On top of this, one would ideally like to master and mobilise the secondary literature on these figures and on their views, which even in the case of Mauss – not to speak of Durkheim – is considerable. To mention just two instances: how far does Durkheim succumb to the temptation of essentialising the sacred (Isambert 1982: 245), and is it true that Mauss's *mana* forms a better basis for a postmodern sociology of religion than Durkheim's sacred (Martelli 1996)?

However, as throughout, my concern is less with a historical understanding of Mauss's views than with putting them to work in new directions. But before we can move to the Indo-European material, we need to situate his picture of the magic-religion contrast within the wider context. Already in 1908 (I: 23–24), reacting to a paper on magic and Roman law, Hubert and Mauss wrote thus:

> One should not oppose magic phenomena to religious phenomena: among religious phenomena there are several systems, that of religion, that of magic, and others too; for instance divination and what is called folklore form systems of religious facts comparable to the previous ones. This classification corresponds better to the complexity of the facts and to the variability of the historical relations between magic and religion.

The point is taken up again in the *Manuel*. We have already cited the passage (*M*: 208) which introduces the distinction between religion in the strict or narrow sense (Mauss uses the Latin *stricto sensu*) and the religion in the broad sense (*lato sensu*). Later, he offers two alternative threefold classifications of religious phenomena: into rites and practices, myths and representations, structures and organisations; or into strict-sense religion, broad-sense religion (including magic and divination) and finally superstitions. It is the second classification that governs his presentation. The 'superstitions' correspond to the 'folklore' of 1908: 'like a great halo around the nuclei formed by magic and religion one finds folklore or popular beliefs' (*M*: 212). 'Around religion *stricto sensu*, around its two great satellites, magic and divination, floats an immense amorphous mass, a nebula,[6] which is the system of popular religion, of popular superstitions' (*M*: 258).

For present purposes we can ignore folklore. What fascinates me is the triad formed by strict-sense religion and its two satellites. As regards the former, one must not overemphasise sacrifice. Hubert and Mauss claimed to have chosen it for their first study because among all religious acts they judged it 'one of the most typical' (04, *SA*: 138);[7] but it was only one order of facts among others. In the introduction to his thesis he compared it world-historically with two other orders of facts. The system of alimentary prohibitions, so highly developed in elementary religions (such as totemism), had regressed to the point of almost complete disappearance. Sacrifice, characteristic of a certain degree of religious development, had tended to lose vitality qua ritual, disappearing from Buddhism, Jainism and official Islam, and surviving in Christianity only in mythic and symbolic form. In contrast, prayer had tended to increase in importance (09, I: 360). In other words, sacrifice was aligned with food rules and with prayer.

When introducing his threefold classification of religious phenomena Mauss sees strict-sense religion as characterised not only by notions of the sacred properly so called, but also by obligations, exactly as juridical phenomena are characterised, whereas the notion of obligation does not intervene in magic or divination (*M*: 212).

If one regrets the loss of Mauss's paper on the relation between religion and magic, one might regret even more the scanty and scrappy quality of the page and a half that he devotes to the third element in his system (*M*: 257–8). Divination is 'a system of representations concerning the future determined as a function of the present and the past', and it 'proceeds with the aid of sympathies, correspondences and *sui generis* forces'. 'Each society possesses its cosmology and its system of classifications, which are proper to it.' 'A classification dominates the whole: correspondences interlink names, animal and vegetable species, conditions (*états*), techniques and activities of all sorts.' In other words, Mauss is here basing divination on cosmological classification. This was an established feature of his thinking: already in 1903 he and Durkheim had introduced the Chinese form of primitive classification as a system that is 'divinatory, astronomical, astrological, geomantic and horoscopic' (03, II: 71). Moreover, they go on to say that it is 'essentially' a system of divination, and to argue that 'nothing is more natural than the relation between divination and the classification of things. At the basis of the system of divination there is a system of classification, at least an implicit one' (II: 78–79).

Put crudely then, Mauss's lecture notes propose a distinction between strict-sense religion and a more embracing concept that relates to classification and cosmology. This will be our main theme in what follows, but before leaving the passage it is worth noting the reference to the relation between divination and shamanism: like the shaman, the diviner can 'travel in the Beyond' (*M*: 258).

A set of journeys

Like any Indologist, Mauss was well aware of the *Mahābhārata*, the great Indian epic. Longer and more inclusive than the *Rāmāyaṇa*, it reached written form around the turn of the eras, but only after a long process of oral transmission which ultimately goes back to proto-Indo-European times. Already as a student he was introduced to the 'Bhagavad Gītā', (part of Book 6 of the *Mahābhārata*) and to the story of Nala and Damayantī (34, III: 538), and he refers to the epics from time to time. Thus, in discussing how myth penetrates legends, he mentions the constant intervention of the gods in the Sanskrit epics (as in the *Iliad* and *Aeneid*), and he also mentions the epics as acceptable authorities to cite in Indian law courts (*M*: 138, 251). In *The Gift* he made considerable use of one of the didactic, non-narrative sections of the *Mahābhārata*, but his references to the main plot hardly go beyond the cryptic statement that the epic is 'the story of a gigantic potlatch; the dice game of the Kauravas against the Pāṇḍavas; the tournament and choice of bridegroom by Draupadī, sister and polyandrous wife of the Pāṇḍavas'[8] (25, *SA*: 243). Whatever Mauss meant by his reference to the potlatch, he here picks out some major features of the plot. After losing the game of dice, the five Pāṇḍavas brothers have to go into exile for twelve years, as is described in Book 3 of the epic, and within this book there take place a number of journeys. Three of them will be of primary interest here.

Let us start with the journey that the reader encounters last. This is the journey to Hell made by Duryodhana, the central character among the usurping Kauravas, who represent the demonic world opposed to the gods. Towards the end of the exile, in the section titled 'The Cattle Expedition', Duryodhana leads his forces out from the capital with a view to gloating over his exiled rivals. However, he provokes a group of lesser supernaturals, is defeated by them, and is rescued by force of arms by Arjuna and the Pāṇḍavas. This humiliation mortifies him so deeply that he decides to starve to death, ignoring the urgings of his friends. Clothed in a skirt of grass and rags, he seats himself on the ground in silence, yearning for Heaven (vB, II: 691).[9] The Dānava demons, worried about their champion, have recourse to rituals and spells drawn from the Atharva Veda. Oblations are made into the fire, from which there arises a wondrous female called Kṛtyā. In response to the demons' commands she takes Duryodhana and enters the nether world, and soon after hands him over to the demons. Urging him to abandon his fast, the demons raise his morale, telling him that he was born from Shiva and that he is divine.[10] Aided by the demons, he and his allies will defeat the Pāṇḍavas. He is embraced by the demons and brought back to earth by Kṛtyā. He does not talk about his trip, which he believes to be a dream, but the next day he abandons his fast and leads his army back to the capital, re-entering it as if in triumph.

I turn now to the first of the three journeys to be narrated (vB, II: 295ff.), which offers an obvious contrast. Not long after the start of the exile, the sage Vyāsa comes to the Pāṇḍavas with instructions that the middle brother, Arjuna, leave them and undertake a journey to Heaven, where he will meet his divine father, Indra, king of the gods. Arjuna goes alone to a Himalayan glade, where he stays for four months, dressed in grass and bark, subjecting himself to extreme fasting and other physical austerities. After receiving visits and help from various gods, he is carried up to Heaven in a celestial chariot which is sent by Indra to collect him. The divine father embraces his son (vB, II: 309), and explains to a visiting sage called Lomaśa that Arjuna is no mere mortal but his (Indra's) own son, as well as being the incarnation of another ancient sage. Arjuna has come to Heaven to ensure the defeat of some powerful Dānava demons, who live in the nether world. The hero conducts a successful solo military campaign against two groups of Dānavas and returns to Heaven. After five years, having received from Indra training, weapons, a crown or diadem, and promises of victory over the Kauravas (vB, II: 552), he is then returned to earth in the chariot. He rejoins his brothers and the exile continues.

These two journeys have been presented extremely concisely and selectively, but however they were presented it would be difficult to overlook the symmetry or parallelism between them. Among the details one notes that both heroes fast in special ascetic garb, and both receive promises of victory. The main point is that the Pāṇḍavas represent the forces of order (*dharma*), and their foremost champion visits the king of the gods in Heaven, while the Kauravas represent the forces of cosmic disorder (*adharma*) and their leader visits the demons in Hell. Admittedly, Arjuna too visits Hell, but this is a sub-episode within his visit to Heaven, and his dealings with the demons who dwell there contrast sharply with those of Duryodhana: rather than receiving their friendly reassurance, he treats the demons as enemies and trounces them.

Recalling Mauss, we see that Duryodhana's journey is surrounded by an aura of magic and is set within a magical milieu.

First, the journey is set in motion by a ritual involving the Atharva Veda, the last of the four collections of Vedic hymns. But when Hubert and Mauss list the sources they use for their work on magic, they reserve special praise for early India: 'The Hindus have provided us with an incomparable body of documents on magic: hymns and magic formulae of the Atharva Veda'.[11]

Secondly, the female produced by the demons' ritual is called Kṛtyā, and this is not just a name. The word is derived from the root *kṛ* 'make, do', and means 'magic' – as Mauss well knew (04, *SA*: 11). Ritual acts, he says:

> are eminently efficacious; they are creative; they make or do things (*ils font*). Magic rites are even more particularly conceived in this way; so much so that they have often taken their name from this efficaciousness. In India the word which corresponds best to the word 'rite' is *karman* 'act'; bewitching is even the *factum*, *kṛtyā* par excellence.[12]

The main point is that the hero is transported by magic.

Thirdly, in the role of transporters of their respective heroes, Kṛtyā the female has as counterpart Indra's charioteer Mātali, who is male. The difference in sex is probably not accidental. Hubert and Mauss comment of the important role accorded to women in magic, at least theoretically, if less so in practice, and they connect it with women's

position in society. This position, both legal and religious, results from
the special qualities attributed to them, qualities that are evidenced by
their menstruation and the mysteries of their reproductive physiology.
'Women constantly give off malign influences. *Nirṛtir hi strī* "women
are death", as the old Brahmanical texts put it' (04, *SA*: 113).[13]

Fourthly, Duryodhana's journey takes place in an atmosphere that
is secretive, shame-faced and disreputable. He has already been
shamed, but suicide would make him a laughing stock of kings: as the
demons say, it is an act of notorious disrepute (vB, II: 691). Demons
themselves are in a sense disreputable, as is the Atharva Veda. The
journey takes place overnight. Duryodhana thinks it is a dream and
keeps it to himself. One almost feels that the bards themselves were
anxious to get through the episode quickly and unobtrusively, giving it
less than forty slokas (couplets) out of the hundred thousand in the
whole epic.

It is in just such an atmosphere that magic operates. As we saw,
Hubert and Mauss presented magic as 'private, secret, mysterious and
tending towards the prohibited'. It is associated with the left hand
rather than the right (as are women), and it tends to be performed at
night or in darkness. Even when licit it hides itself. The magician's acts
may be furtive, his words indistinct, the whole event enveloped in mys-
tery and scarcely respectable, *peu estimable* (04, *SA*: 15–16). It is
somewhat on the margins of legality (*M*: 256).

Fifthly, the demons claim to have obtained Duryodhana from Shiva
by practising austerities, and his body is imbued with Shiva and
Shiva's female counterpart Devī (vB, II: 692). Mauss mentions just
this god in his paragraph on magical cults. Since the argument is that
magic is not part of an organised cult, magical cults are held to be secondary developments, arising when magicians follow the lead set by
religion. The examples cited are 'the cults of Hecate in Greek magic, of
Diana and the devil in the magic of the Middle Ages, and one whole
part of the cult of one of the greatest Hindu gods, Rudra-Shiva' (04,
SA: 16).

Finally, when the demons say that Duryodhana is imbued with
Shiva and Devī, they are building on what they have just said, namely
that the upper part of the hero's body was made of piles of diamonds
and (hence) is invulnerable, while the lower was made by Devī out of
flowers and is seductive to women for its beauty. The composition of
Duryodhana's lower body relates to his attempted seduction of Draupadī in Book 2 and to his mode of death (the second brother, Bhīma,
crushes his thigh), but it also reflects Shiva's *ardhanarīśvara* image, in
which the god's left half is female, his right half male. Such bisexual-
ity is important in Hindu alchemy, whose symbols come from the
Shaivite tradition (White 1997: 75–77). Thus in the closely related

hathayoga tradition, the subtle body is vertically bisected. 'All that lies above the navel is male, and thereby identified with male seed, with the moon that exudes vivifying nectar, and [with] the god Shiva . . . All that lies below the navel is female, identified with female uterine or menstrual blood, with the sun that provides the thermal energy necessary to fuel the transformation of seed into nectar, and [with] the goddess Śakti' (who is regularly identified with Devī). All this recalls the linkage made by Hubert and Mauss between magic and the female, and accords with their remarks on the relation of magic to alchemy (*SA*: 135–6).

Arjuna's journey also seems straightforward. A visit to Heaven and a welcome from the head of the pantheon surely connote religion? Elements of secrecy and isolation are not wholly absent: Arjuna receives from Vyāsa, via his eldest brother Yudhiṣṭhira, secret magic knowledge called Siddhi (vB, II: 295–6), which apparently helps him reach the Himalayas, and his austerities are conducted solo. Moreover, the first deity he encounters is Shiva, who after defeating him in a duel helps his onward progress. However, all this is preliminary, and once the chariot arrives to take him to Heaven he soon finds himself, as it were, in a blaze of publicity. He passes the multitudinous stars, which are actually the luminous spirits of humans who have reached Heaven, and is driven along the path of the gods, receiving praise and welcome from gods, sages and supernaturals of all sorts. Enthroned in the royal assembly hall, he enjoys celestial music and dance. The text seems to emphasise the publicity of the arrival, and it gives the whole of Arjuna's journey some 700 slokas. Although the greater part of this is third-person narrative, almost half is in first-person form: far from trying to keep his journey a secret, Arjuna narrates it at length to his brothers. He narrates it again to Krishna when the latter visits the exiles (vB, II: 571–2), and it is not very long before the news reaches the blind king of the Kauravas (vB, II: 674). There is nothing shamefaced about this journey.

One is therefore strongly tempted to align the contrast between Arjuna's journey and Duryodhana's with the contrast between religion and magic. As for the vertical dimension, when they contrast the two poles of sacrifice and malefice, Hubert and Mauss talk of religion as always creating 'a sort of ideal towards which hymns, vows and sacrifices *ascend* [my italics], and which is protected by prohibitions. These regions are avoided by magic' (*SA*: 14). They themselves avoid any formulation so crude as religion : magic :: Heaven : Hell :: up : down, which would only fit certain cultures, but the orientation of the two journeys in the Indian case would surely not have surprised them.

However, when we take account of our third journey, this binary analysis ceases to satisfy.

When the sage Lomaśa visits Heaven and asks Indra about Arjuna's presence there, Indra not only satisfies his curiosity but also issues him with instructions. The sage is to go to earth, find Yudhiṣṭhira, give him news of Arjuna, and tell him to take his party on a pilgrimage around the sacred fords of India.[14] After bathing in them, the Pāṇḍavas will be freed from evil, and they will (eventually) recover the throne. Lomaśa is to guard the party against demons by the power of his religious austerities. (vB, II: 311)

Meanwhile, the Pāṇḍavas on earth are sorely missing Arjuna, and passing the time by listening to the story of Nala and Damayantī. Another sage arrives and the conversation turns towards pilgrimage, which can bring even greater rewards than sacrifice (vB, II: 374), and which should sometimes be combined with fasting. The Pāṇḍavas' chaplain takes up the theme of sacred fords, and finally Lomaśa arrives with Indra's instructions to Yudhiṣṭhira. Further sages appear, exhorting the pilgrims to purity and conferring blessings. Together with Lomaśa and a number of brahmans, the party sets off wearing bark and deerskins (vB, II: 407).

The pilgrimage then takes them clockwise around India (conventionally expressed as 'following the course of the sun'): they set out eastwards, and end up in the north, in the Himalayas, where they are reunited with Arjuna. The pilgrimage covers much the same ground as Arjuna himself in Book 1 when he travelled round India, ostensibly as a penance. The Book 3 story is told at considerable length, being padded out with inserted stories weakly linked to the main plot. Shrine after shrine is visited, and sometimes austerities are practised. Thus in the western quarter Yudhiṣṭhira lives on water and wind for twelve days (vB, II: 449), and when Krishna visits him there he is lying on the ground in his bark cloth.

What is the relation between the pilgrimage and Arjuna's celestial journey? Both are set in motion by sages who arrive with instructions and assistance – one imagines Vyāsa is following instructions from Indra, as Lomaśa is doing explicitly. Both journeys at some point involve austerities. However, the pilgrimage does not include a meeting between Yudhiṣṭhira and his divine father Dharma, a meeting which only occurs at the very end of Book 3. On the other hand, the trips overlap in time, though the celestial journey starts before the earthly one and lasts a little longer (pilgrim activity seems to cease a little before the reunion). Moreover, the journeys are causally linked since the pilgrimage is partly undertaken in order to cope with the Pāṇḍavas' sense of desolation in the absence of their much loved middle brother. These points suggest that the two journeys are to be seen as parallel, but less so than the journeys of Arjuna and Duryodhana. Using the framework of the Indo-European functions, we shall later suggest an explanation.

One thing is obvious: like any pilgrimage, this is a religious journey. The whole atmosphere is religious in the narrow sense: sacred bathing places, sages, chaplains, brahmans. The atmosphere strikes one all the more forcibly when one reflects that the episode comes in an epic centering on a great war, and that Yudhiṣṭhira, the future king, is a Kṣatriya (warrior) by birth. But to make full sense of it, we need to enlarge the picture further, and take account of three other journeys in Book 3. Although all three accounts are relatively short (though less so than the journey to Hell), the evidence is still complex, and the accounts will be even more compressed than those of the three main journeys.

After the pilgrims reach the Himalayas, and before their reunion with Arjuna, their progress from shrine to shrine is twice interrupted by journeys that are extremely similar. In both cases the wind blows flowers to the Pāṇḍavas. Draupadī desires them and sends Bhīma on a one-day journey to where they grow (whence my name – the two 'flower journeys'). Bhīma takes his weapons, hastens uphill, fights demons, and is finally rejoined by the rest of the party. Both journeys end with references to Kubera, the god of wealth, in whose territory the party find themselves. On the first journey Bhīma also encounters his elder brother, the monkey god Hanuman.

After the reunion with Arjuna the party move back to the plains, and then follows the last journey we need to mention. Taking his bow and sword, Bhīma goes to the jungle on an expedition to hunt deer, and encounters a hungry boa constrictor who is a metamorphosis of Nahuṣa, a Pāṇḍava ancestor who once occupied Indra's throne. The snake, who is even stronger than Bhīma, imprisons the hero in his coils and is only induced to release him by Yudhiṣṭhira correctly answering his questions. Nahuṣa resumes his celestial form and returns to Heaven, while Bhīma accompanies his older brother back to the hermitage where they are staying (vB, II: 567). A number of relationships link the 'boa journey' with the first flower journey – for instance, both Hanuman and the boa prove stronger than the strongest Pāṇḍava.

For reasons of space and balance I cannot convincingly demonstrate that these six journeys constitute an exhaustive set. The full argument would have to examine in some detail the only other obvious main-plot journey undertaken by heroes within Book 3, which comes right at its end. A brahman conducting a fire sacrifice suffers the loss of his ritual instruments when a deer catches them in its antlers and runs off to a lake. Yudhiṣṭhira is asked by the brahman to retrieve the implements and eventually succeeds. It turns out that the deer is one of the disguises adopted by Yudhiṣṭhira's divine father Dharma in order to test his son. Like the pilgrimage, which also focused on the eldest Pāṇḍava, the 'fire-sticks' or 'lake' journey takes place in a pervasively religious atmosphere – brahman, sacrificial ritual, Dharma, dharmic behaviour. In that sense it is closely related to the pilgrimage, but we need not decide exactly how – whether for instance as a separated fragment or as an alternative version.

Interpretation in terms of Indo-European ideology

To understand all this narrative material we have to return to the topic of the Indo-European primitive classification. As we saw in Ch. 6, there is now a good deal of evidence for the view that proto-Indo-European culture made pervasive use of a systematic pentadic classification, each class (in the 'vertical' sense) being defined by a distinct bundle of ideas. The bundles, which were ranked, have come to be called functions. The numerical labels they have been given express this rank and the history of recognition of the classes, together with the fact that the sequence can sometimes be seen as cyclical. Hence from highest rank to lowest the sequence is 4+,1,2,3,4–. The central triad or core can be thought of as pertaining respectively to the priestly or sacred, to physical force and warriors, to fecundity, prosperity and producers, while the fourth function is defined as pertaining to what is other, outside or beyond relative to the core. It is divided into two halves: positive, valued and transcendent, versus negative, devalued and excluded, which can be conveniently thought of as king versus slave. The abstract pentadic pattern constituted the ideology, and was manifested in numerous different contexts such as myths and other narratives, laws, rituals, stereotypical social structure. Both the ideology and particular manifestations of it were spread across time and space predominantly in and alongside the Indo-European languages, so that manifestations of the pattern turn up in most parts of the Indo-European linguistic world. However, over the course of centuries or millennia, the pattern tended to blur or fade out, so that manifestations became fewer and more tenuous.

As I have argued elsewhere, the Sanskrit epic is particularly rich in instances of the ancient pattern. One such instance is provided by the 'dynasts', the central figures in the dynastic conflict at the heart of the epic. Those who believe that there are only three functions have long argued that this pattern is represented by the five Pāṇḍavas. Of course, all the brothers belong to the warrior *varṇa* or estate (second function), but nonetheless they show contrasting orientations. In order of their birth, Yudhiṣṭhira is the pious son of Dharma and represents F1, Bhīma and Arjuna are the warriors par excellence (F2) and the youngest brothers, the twins Nakula and Sahadeva, represent the relatively humble F3. If one accepts a bifurcated fourth function (for which there are many entirely independent arguments), the picture changes. From a Pāṇḍava perspective, the enemy par excellence is Duryodhana, who qualifies as F4–. The F4+ position is more problematic, but many reasons combine to suggest that Arjuna belongs here, rather than in F2 (Allen 1999a). For instance, his birth story is quite different from that of Bhīma and the others, his orientation is less easy to delimit than theirs, and during the thirteenth year of exile, which the Pāṇḍavas have to spend incognito, Arjuna's disguise hardly fits F2. In these and other respects, he is best seen as standing outside the sequence of brothers and transcending them as a king transcends his subjects. After the great battle, it is Yudhiṣṭhira who actually becomes king, but Arjuna is again and again the 'symbolic king', as Biardeau and others have noted. Thus in the table below he has been placed firmly under F4+.

Interestingly, if one turns from the dynasts to the generals they employ, the numerical relations are reversed. Among the dynasts there are five Pāṇḍavas versus Duryodhana, while the Kauravas have five successive generals (themselves filling the five slots in the ideology), the Pāṇḍavas only one (Allen 1999b). I mention this partly as exemplifying the sort of aesthetic effect in which the epic specialises (Mauss always attached great importance to the aesthetic), partly because it provides another instance of the sort of interpretation that is called for if we are to make sense of the set of journeys in Book 3.

The question then is whether the journeys can be associated with the dynasts and/or with the functions. The journeys need to be conceptualised and labelled, then looked at from several points of view: who travels or leads the travellers; what supernaturals and/or relatives this individual most saliently meets; what is the purpose of the journey; what atmosphere, if any, characterises it. This information, with a few simplifications or short cuts, is tabulated below.

functions	F4+	F1	F2	F3	F4–
dynasts	Arjuna	Yudhiṣṭhira	Bhīma	twins	Duryodhana
journeys[15]	to Heaven	pilgrimage/lake	flower journeys 1/2	boa	to Hell
terrestrial?	extra-terrestrial	terrestrial	terrestrial	terrestrial	extra-terrestrial
traveller	Arjuna	Yudhiṣṭhira	Bhīma/Bhīma	Bhīma	Duryodhana
encounters	Indra	–/Dharma	Hanuman/Kubera	Nahuṣa	Demons
purpose	cosmic order	purification	flowers/flowers	hunting	*adharma*
atmosphere	religious?	religious	(not easily characterised)		magic

It is clear at once from the tabulation that in the F2–3 columns the entries for the journeys present many anomalies. I cannot discuss these journeys in the detail they merit, but to ignore them altogether would weaken the main argument. We are operating in a delicate area. When the conformity of a narrative to a preconceived pattern is not patent, the analyst who postulates historical change from an earlier situation where the fit was better risks the accusation of tendentiousness. But such changes must sometimes occur, and all one can do is proceed in full awareness of the dangers.

The two flower journeys are 'twinned': they are so clearly like each other that students have tended to take them as older and newer versions of the same story that have somehow found their way into a single text. But among the dynasts the third function is represented by twins. Moreover, the twins are missing in the traveller row, while the F2 Bhīma, who has no particular appropriateness as a collector of flowers, is 'over-represented'. This prompts the hypothesis that Bhīma has displaced the humble twins, who originally undertook or led one of the flower journeys each. Two points support this idea. First, on both occasions the flowers are explicitly beautiful, and they appeal particularly to Draupadī. Draupadī is a young woman, and whether she wants the flowers to decorate the hermitage or to beautify herself, the conjunction of femininity and beauty hints at sexuality. Both beauty and sexuality (*volupté*) are included in the full definition of the third function (Dumézil 1958: 19), and the matchless male beauty of the twins is their distinctive characteristic in the Pāṇḍava birth stories (Allen 1999a: 406). Secondly, both flower journeys end with references to Kubera, the god of wealth, who elsewhere appears as an F3 representative among the gods of the cardinal points (Allen 1999b: 247–49).

Neither Kubera nor questions of beauty have any place in Bhīma's boa journey. This is a hunting expedition, an entirely approprate undertaking for a brother whose exceptionally muscular physique goes with a gargantuan appetite. Since there is a tendency (admittedly not invariable) for manifestations of the four-functional ideology to conform to the canonical order, one might imagine that in an earlier phase of the tradition some such hunting expedition preceded the flower journeys. The encounter with Hanuman, whose affiliations are much more with F2 than with F3, has no obvious connection with the search for the flowers, and could be a survival from this earlier phase, while the encounter with Nahuṣa in boa form would be a variant version of the same story. However, I need not pursue these historical questions further. In the text as we have it, the F2–3 journeys are not devoid of religious elements – for instance, Hanuman instructs Bhīma in the history of *dharma* and Nahuṣa and Yudhiṣṭhira exchange questions and answers on religious topics. However, although the old ideology seems to be somewhat blurred, it is fair to say at least that these episodes are not directed by the magico-religious preoccupations so

characteristic of the three remaining journeys. It is on these, which fit
the schema so neatly, that my main argument focuses.[16]

Within this triad the two F4 journeys are rather closely parallel,
both of them being solo and extraterrestrial in contrast to the pilgrimage. But the connection between Duryodhana and F4–, and between
Duryodhana's journey and magic, are relatively clear, and the main
problem concerns the other two columns. I shall mostly take for
granted the interpretation of Arjuna as F4+ and Yudhiṣṭhira as F1,
and focus on the connection between their journeys and the notion of
religion.

As we saw, pilgrimage is presented by the epic as even more meritorious than sacrifice, which Hubert and Mauss selected as among the
most typical of religious acts. Ever since the 1940s trifunctionalists
have recognised Yudhiṣṭhira as the F1 representative among the
Pāṇḍavas, emphasising his birth from Dharma, the announcement at
his birth that he will be the greatest of all upholders of *dharma*, his
decision to disguise himself as a brahman for the thirteenth year, and
his generally pious, dutiful and unwarlike character. There is every
reason to associate his pilgrimage, with or without the lake journey,
with religion in the strict sense.

It would be hard to maintain that Arjuna's journey was *not* religious. On the instructions of a sage, conveyed to him via his F1 elder
brother, he is ritually consecrated before setting out, and his journey is
blessed by brahmans (vB, II: 296). He travels by Indrayoga, and
attracts the attention of Shiva by austerities such as are often practised
by holy men. He has contacts with a sequence of deities on earth and
with deities *en masse* in Heaven. The battle for which he needs the
weapons provided by Indra and the other gods is part of the ongoing
moral struggle between gods, supporters of *dharma*, and demons.

On the other hand, Arjuna himself is a 'symbolic king' and the
quintessence of the warrior estate. In other contexts he seldom shows
more than the proper respect a warrior owes to religion, and his celestial journey is overtly directed to obtaining weapons, not religious
merit. To assimilate it to a pilgrimage seems crude. In other words, we
shall need some sort of distinction between the undertakings of the
two brothers, parallel to that between F4+ and F1. But since 'religious'
applies so well to the undertaking of the elder brother, we need a different term for Arjuna's. I suggest cosmological.

Although Arjuna's journey is primarily celestial, actually it covers
the whole cosmos: as we saw, it includes a journey to the nether world,
and the opening part of the journey, as far as the Himalayas, is terrestrial. This opening transit may seem too slight to relate to the terrestrial level of the cosmos but, firstly, Arjuna has already visited the four
corners of the subcontinent during his 'penance' in Book 1, and

secondly, although he does not repeat this circumambulation, the ter-restrial part of his journey culminates in an event that is comparable. This time, instead of his visiting the cardinal points, the gods of the cardinal points come to visit him and to give him their gifts or promises. So his journey brings him into contact both with the zenith, nadir and terrestrial directions, which is to say, symbolically, with the whole of space. In this respect he obviously contrasts with the other dynasts. Of the remaining Pāṇḍavas, none ever visits Hell, and Dury-odhana never makes an earthly pilgrimage; nor do any of them go to Heaven until after their deaths (in Book 18, at the end of the epic).

Since parts are transcended by wholes, F4+ is often manifested in references to totality, and the spatial dimension is only one of the ways in which Arjuna and his journey are associated with totalities. The goal is Indra, and Yudhiṣṭhira tells his younger brother that Indra pos-sesses all the weapons of the gods, that the gods gave Indra all their strength: 'You will find all the weapons assembled there in one place.' Arjuna is accessing the totality of divine force.

But Arjuna is not only to gain military might. When Vyāsa conveys his secret spell Siddhi to Yudhiṣṭhira, he implies that if Arjuna will be able to see the gods it is because in some sense he is Nara, the ancient seer and divinity, one of a pair with Nārāyaṇa or Vishnu. This fre-quently mentioned facet of Arjuna's being cannot be explored here, but the notion of Arjuna's journey as that of a seer is interesting. When Siddhi is passed on to him, Arjuna learns that if he uses it 'the entire world will become visible to him'. In other words, he is to gain cosmic clairvoyance. The text does not tell us how or when he exer-cised this power, though perhaps hints can be found in his viewing of the stars and of the gods' park or parks (vB, II: 308, 542) during his celestial chariot ride.

In addition to these spatial and cognitive senses of totality one can probably recognise a theological sense. The public reception of Arjuna, with its lists of supernaturals and its reference to chariots of the gods numbered in thousands and tens of thousands (vB, II: 309), implies that he is welcomed by the totality of supernaturals, excluding demons. Secondly, Mātali tells him that Indra wants the 'thirty celes-tials' to be present (vB, II: 307), and this figure, used instead of the full 'thirty-three', implies the pantheon as a whole. Finally, it is no accident that in the course of his journey Arjuna deals with precisely five deities. As the list stands at present, there is not a perfect fit between these five and the functions, but the figure can again be read as imply-ing a totality.

We need also to look at the temporal relationships. The five-year duration of Arjuna's journey includes or encompasses the whole of Yudhiṣṭhira's pilgrimage and both flower journeys. It does not include the boa journey but, as we saw, the latter is apparently anticipated by the encounter with Hanuman during the first flower journey. On the hypothesis presented above, Arjuna's five-year absence would originally have covered the journeys of the four other brothers.

It is worth pursuing this idea just a little further. As we saw, the pentad of Pāṇḍava dynasts corresponds to a pentad of successive Kaurava generals distributed across the functions in the standard order. The length of each generals' tenure forms a steadily decreasing series, from ten days down to one night. General I, Bhīṣma, retires when disabled and only dies well after the eighteen-day battle, whereas generals II, III, and IV all die during the battle. Thus a parallel exists between the F4+ general Bhīṣma, who outlives his F1–3 successors, and the F4+ dynast, Arjuna, whose journey (on our hypothesis) encompasses those of his F1–3 brothers. General V outlives Bhīṣma, albeit as a despicable outsider, somewhat as Duryodhana's journey definitely falls outside Arjuna's five years.[17]

Of course, Mauss did not analyse this particular stretch of the Indian epic, and even if he had, he would not have had available the mental tool of the expanded Dumézilian schema, with its five-slot primitive classification. Nevertheless, he was aware of several of the elements that have gone into the analysis above, and his formulations sometimes approach this. Above all, he saw that religion in the narrow sense, of which sacrifice was so typical, had two satellites, not just one – that is, the magic that had for so long been paired and contrasted with religion. Even his choice of the label 'divination' for this third element in broad-sense religion is not inappropriate to Arjuna's case. Arjuna is a seer or rishi who goes to the other world, and comes back with knowledge of the future in the form of the promises made to him by the ruler of the cosmos, in addition to pronouncements made by other deities. 'Even the multitudes of gods cannot vanquish you in battle', let alone other humans (vB, II: 543, 552). The same message is conveyed by Indra directly to Yudhiṣṭhira immediately after Arjuna's return (vB, II: 538), but that does not detract from the element of divination in Arjuna's journey.

As we saw, even in his very brief treatment of divination Mauss finds space to connect it with shamanism and otherworldly journeys. Arjuna's journey is conducted with the aid of 'Indrayoga', and in various other ways relates to the undertaking of the yogin; but yogic spiritual ascents are no doubt interiorised forms of shamanic journeys, as is suggested by the comparison between Arjuna's journey to Heaven and Odysseus' journey from Ogygia to Scheria (Allen 1998c).[18]

When summarising Mauss's remarks on divination, we also noted his emphasis on classifications and cosmology. Parts of the relevant passage were quoted earlier, before we examined Arjuna's journey, but here is another, of similar tenor. Under the heading of divination the investigator will study 'questions pertaining to cosmological allotments, coincidences in time and space, the distribution of stars' (*M*: 258). Arjuna does indeed receive instruction about the nature of stars – admittedly not about their distribution in constellations, though the story could easily accommodate such information. More important is the cosmic and spatial dimension of the journey, which we have already tried to relate to time as well as to the pantheon. In the last analysis, however, the whole discussion has been about the functions, which is to say about a system of primitive classification. I repeat Mauss's comment about divination: 'classification dominates this ensemble'.

I argued in Chapter 6 that, although Mauss tended to align class (*genre*) with the other categories, it actually enjoys a certain priority, and is more fundamental than at least some of the others. We now see that from an Indo-European point of view this priority makes sense. However we approach the matter, we are dealing with a single set of interrelated notions: Arjuna's journey, cosmological religion, primitive classifications, totalities, the fourth function in its valued aspect. One can enter the set at any point and find connections in all directions.

We must not exaggerate Mauss's prescience. He was very far from an adequate theorisation of his distinction between strict-sense religion and his 'divination'. In the *Manuel* much material relating to shamanism, primitive classification and categories appears under strict-sense religion, especially in the subsection on the representations of the beings and phenomena of nature (*M*: 246–48).[19] If the Sanskrit material is a safe guide, and if we are on the right track, Mauss ought to have shifted this material to the divination section and renamed the latter 'cosmology'. He would then scarcely have called it a 'satellite' of strict-sense religion.

Auspicia and sacra

The *Mahābhārata* is a treasury of four-functional patterns, and some of them are both very old and very well preserved – as the comparisons with the Greek and to some extent Celtic materials indicate. The age of the pattern formed by the dynasts' journeys is beyond our scope here, but if the distinction between F4+ and F1 is a general feature of Indo-European ideology, one would expect to find it applied to broad-sense religion in other parts of the Indo-European world. Dumézil's original recognition of the functions arose from a comparison between Sanskrit and Roman materials, so let us turn to the latter. I draw heavily on Allen 1996b, which gives fuller references.[20]

From 1945 onwards Dumézil frequently cited a passage from

Cicero's *De Natura Deorum* (3.5). The crucial statement is that 'the whole religion (*omnis religio*) of the Roman people is divided (*divisa sit*) into *sacra* and *auspicia*'. If *sacra* cover sacrifices and other priestly ritual, *auspicia* cover methods of divination – etymologically it refers to the observation of the flight of birds (*aves*). The text goes on to mention further divinatory methods that were added on (*adiunctum*) as a third component, but it then reverts to the pairing: 'Romulus, by establishing the *auspicia*,[21] Numa by establishing the *sacra*, laid the foundations of our state, which could certainly never have become so great had it not enjoyed the highest favour of the gods'. The adjunct third component is not here linked to a king.

Romulus is of course the founder of Rome and its first king, while Numa was his successor. Dumézil makes much of this pairing, arguing in his mature work that the first two kings both represent the first function, and that their successors Tullus and Ancus represent the second and third functions. The postulated split within the first function is not confined to this particular context but recurs elsewhere. In Rome itself it is seen again in the juxtaposition of Jupiter and Fides (or her male relative Dius Fidius), while Scandinavia offers Odin and Tyr and above all, India has the Vedic gods Varuṇa and Mitra. This pair give their names to the two aspects of the first function, on which Dumézil presents his definitive views in 1977.[22] Reviewing the contrast between the two gods, he offers as a summary that 'Mitra is closer to man, Varuṇa less close', closeness being understood in a broad sense that includes friendship. We need not list all the facets of the contrast, but here are a few useful points. 'Mitra is this world, Varuṇa is the other world', as the *Śatapatha Brāhmaṇa* puts it. Mitra tends to gentleness and juridical methods, Varuṇa tends to violence. Of the two Mitra is linked with *bráhman*, the principle of the priestly first function, while Varuṇa is more saliently a king (1977: 61–79).[23]

Using the same framework Dumézil then contrasts the ambitious and violent Romulus with the peaceful, sage-like, law-minded figure of Numa (1977: 159–66). The passage from Cicero is cited with the following discussion:

> The art of *auspicia* consists in sometimes seeking, always receiving and interpreting, occasionally rejecting the signs that the great god sends to men; the art of *sacra* is the cult maintained by humanity, with its prayers, negotiations and offerings. Thus in religious interaction *auspicia* and *sacra* define the two directions, the two points of departure and also the two styles: the former come from the other world into this one, the latter are carried out on earth and go to the gods; faced by the former, humanity is on the receiving end, while with the latter, if one is not afraid of modern images, it is the broadcaster; the former are mysterious, often anxiety-provoking or unpredicted, the latter follow a [ritual] technique that is entirely clear. (1977: 161)

Roughly speaking then, *auspicia* are to the other world as *sacra* are to this, and the contrast accords with that between the two kings. Romulus, son of a god, and himself divinised at death, even if he has children, is not regarded as a physical ancestor to the Romans, and in these various ways appears as standing outside ordinary humanity. Numa is wholly human and is emphatically an ancestor. One should not oversimplify the comparison with Varuṇa and Mitra, and I doubt whether it is enough simply to argue that the Vedic gods contrast as F4+ to F1 (if only because the two are so closely coupled, and because in the set of gods linked with cardinal points Varuṇa represents F1). But as regards the Roman kings the contrast can reasonably be expressed in those functional terms. Numa is as clear a first-functional figure as one could wish, while Romulus is altogether more complex. For instance he connotes totality in that his name refers to the city as a whole, and as deified founder he lives throughout its history in a sense that does not apply to his wholly human successors.

The four-function approach supplies two further arguments in favour of interpreting Romulus as F4+. Firstly Dumézil's analysis stops short with Ancus, the fourth king, and ignores the final triad, the two Tarquins bracketing the slave king Servius. But these 'outsiders' can be interpreted as representing F4–, and hence as completing the series that starts with Romulus.[24] Secondly, if the whole mythic history of monarchical Rome is patterned by the four functions, so is the founder's own biography, and the first two of its five phases seem to be characterised by *auspicia* and *sacra* respectively (Allen 1996b:23 ff.).

Though Mauss does not apparently refer to the Cicero passage, it is likely that he had read it, either in the original or in the books on religion that he reviewed or otherwise perused. In any case, it accords excellently with his view that divination constituted a set of phenomena distinct from the strict-sense religion so well exemplified by sacrifice. Moreover, the passage gains further significance from the fact that our word 'religion' derives from the Latin.

Truth and sacrifice

For trifunctionalists in general, the Mitra-Varuṇa opposition has been the usual way of conceptualising binary splits within what they interpret as the first function, but there is one comparable split that has been regarded as idiosyncratic. It comes in the story of Yayāti, son of the Nahuṣa mentioned above, a story that is told twice in the *Mahābhārata*. Dumézil has compared the various versions, and I summarise his account (1971: 272ff.).

Yayāti's daughter Mādhavī has sexual relations in turn with four men. She is told that she has borne 'one son who is royal in generosity, another who is a hero, a third who is dedicated to truth and Law, and one more who is a sacrificer' (vB, III: 410). Of the first-born, Vasumanas, it was said at his birth that he would become richer than the Vasus (a class of gods, but *vasu* means 'wealth'); he can be generous because he is so wealthy. If Vasumanas represents the third function, Pratardana the hero (*śura*) represents the second, and that leaves two candidates for the first. Aṣṭaka the sacrificer makes an entirely natural and typical figure, while Śibi the truthful is less typical. Nevertheless Dumézil interprets Śibi as representing the moral aspect of the first function, where Aṣṭaka represents the religious and practical aspect.

The story continues. After a meritorious reign as a universal sovereign, Yayāti resigns the throne and retires to the forest. Undertaking austerities reminiscent of Arjuna's, he ascends to Heaven and enjoys celestial bliss. But pride comes before a fall: his merit is exhausted and he is detected in a moment of arrogance. Cast out from Heaven, he falls towards the spot where his four grandchildren are celebrating a *vājapeya* ritual around a sacred fire. They offer him their merits so that he can regain Heaven. In one account the merits offered derive clearly from the specific natures of the half-brothers – generosity, martial prowess, truth-telling and sacrifice.

While the group are talking, Aṣṭaka sees five chariots appear in the sky (vB, I: 209). The group mount them and as they all ascend heavenwards Śibi's chariot draws ahead, and Aṣṭaka asks Yayāti why: 'I thought I would be first'. Yayāti makes it clear that Śibi is the best of the five.

With his usual acuteness Dumézil senses the awkwardness in interpreting Śibi as F1. As he says, this interpretation of truthfulness does not accord with ordinary Hindu conceptions, and an explanation may be needed that is not available at the present stage of research. On top of the other evidence, when Yayāti lists his own merits, he makes the list climax with 'truth', and:

> the suspicion therefore arises that this fourth source of merit, which complicates the distribution of the whole set over the three functions and almost disguises its structure, is not of the same nature as the other three, but dominates or conditions them. We should have before us the merits of the three functions and, above them, the even more valuable merit of truth-telling, of the absence of lying. (1971: 289–90)

Elsewhere, in a study linking the myth with the Vedic *vājapeya* ritual, Dumézil comments again on the various types of merit in the story. Three of them correspond to the three functional levels, but truthfulness is an addition or annex (*attachement*) 'which no doubt transcends the three functions' (1975: 134). This last formulation accords perfectly with the four-function approach.

However, one further question arises. Since there are five chariots in the story, one for each participant, is there a representative of F4–? The obvious answer is Yayāti, who, though he was once a universal sovereign, is now totally devoid of merits and is heading for a 'terrestrial hell'. In one version he is suddenly treated as an outcaste by the denizens of Heaven: he is divested of his rank, his garlands are withered, his diadem (equivalent to a crown) has fallen, his ornaments and robe are awry (vB, III: 411). More fundamentally, the fateful moment of pride can be interpreted as a lie. Either inwardly or in words he formulates the view that he excels the supernaturals, seers and men around him; and this view is false, an offence against the closely related notions of truth and cosmic order. Dumézil (1971) discusses the point with reference to Iranian materials, comparing Yayāti with the Avestan and post-Avestan figure of Yima. I propose then that in this particular story, the 'Uttara-Yayāti', Śibi represents F4+ and Yayāti F4–.[25]

This story needs to be compared with the six journeys. When Śibi draws ahead in the 'race', one recalls how Arjuna's ascent to Heaven anticipates that of all the dynasts at the end of the epic. Yayāti's hellward journey is due to his own self-destructive thoughts or words, much as is Duryodhana's. Above all, one notes in both cases the complex relationship between the occupants of the two highest-ranking positions. The picture is complicated because in the 'Uttara-Yayāti' the order of birth more or less reverses the standard descending hierarchical order of the functions. Yayāti (F4–) comes first, then two generations later the half-brothers Vasumanas (F3), Pratardana (F2), Śibi and Aṣṭaka. This is the order in which the quartet are typically presented in the text, and if initiatives are not taken by the first-born they are taken by the youngest. Thus in Book 1 it is Aṣṭaka who sees Yayāti falling, who dialogues with him for several pages, who first sees the five chariots, and thinks he ought to have priority in the celestial journey. But Śibi, although he is third-born and not at the end of the sequence, has priority over the youngest. Compare Arjuna, third-born of the Pāṇḍavas. Since the priority in succession to the throne belongs to the eldest, Yudhiṣṭhira, Arjuna never becomes king, but he seems to be a symbolic king and is the first to visit Heaven. More generally, one thinks of the complex relationship between priesthood and kingship in Hindu tradition.

The manifestation of the F1/F4+ opposition is less complex in the Roman material we considered. As founder of the *auspicia*, Romulus is comparable to Śibi, the champion of truthfulness, while Numa, the founder of the *sacra*, parallels Aṣṭaka, the champion of sacrifice.

However, in this case there is no equivocation about relative rank: Romulus is indisputably prior in time and higher in rank.

As Dumézil shows, to make the most of the Yayāti story one has to relate it to the metaphysics of truth and lying in the Indo-Iranian world, to explore the opposition between truth as an aspect of cosmic order (*ṛta* in Sanskrit and the cognate *aša* in Avestan) and falsehood as an aspect of cosmic disorder. It is, of course, no accident that the prophecies received on the extraterrestrial journeys are so different in value. When Indra tells Arjuna that he cannot be overcome by any mortal, he is telling the truth, while the demons' prophecy to Duryodhana that 'the earth will be yours to enjoy without rivals' is false. But truth is not only what actually exists and is the case: *ṛta*, from a verb meaning 'arrange, harmonise', expresses the fact that truth is what is in conformity with cosmic order, with the arrangement of the world and of society. We are not far from primitive classifications, and can perhaps see a little more clearly the scope of cosmic religion.

Beyond the Indo-Europeans

Partly because Mauss was developing an intellectual tradition whose roots are largely Indo-European, partly because he was a Sanskritist and partly because of my own current interests, this chapter has concentrated on India and the wider Indo-European world. Dumézil's trifunctional approach focused on the same region, and although he willingly accepted that trifunctional patterns could be found sporadically elsewhere, for instance in Japan or Africa, he doubted whether these latter were manifestations of a systematic or pervasive ideology. Four-function theory retains the same basic assumptions, and no claim is being made that the four-function ideology is in any way universal. On the contrary, it is envisaged as bounded in space and time. The argument has been that, whether one starts with Mauss's threefold classification of non-folklore religious phenomena, or with the framework of the Indo-European functions, there is a significant fit between the two. The gap between Mauss's divination and his strict-sense religion fits well with the gap between F4+ and F1. The fit was illustrated by the three case studies.

However, the meaning of the fit needs clarification. It might have arisen because Mauss had read his Cicero or was in some other way influenced by the Indo-European intellectual tradition, and proposed his particular classification of religious phenomena as a result. While this could be part of the explanation, another idea seems more likely. In the *Manuel* Mauss was drawing on his world-wide ethnographic knowledge and addressing an audience potentially interested in any region. So perhaps his formulations arose primarily from his general knowledge, and if the Indo-Europeans fit, it is because, in the relevant respects, they are typical and conform to widespread patterns. The argument can be presented from at least two points of view, which can be associated respectively with the categories of totality and class.

In principle an element is never to be construed as F4+ unless it is coordinate with four other elements filling the remaining slots in the ideology. We can recall from Chapter 2 above, the rules for establishing that it is coordinate: the elements in a trifunctional set should not only conform one-for-one to the definitions of the functions, but should also be solidary, homogeneous, distinct and exhaustive. These requirements carry over to four-functional theory, needing only a certain relativisation of the homogeneity requirement. Representatives of F4 must in some sense(s) be heterogeneous relative to the central triad, but in some other(s) they must be homogeneous. The requirements are fairly strict, and it would be surprising if they were often met outside the Indo-European world. However, the valued otherness that defines F4+ often takes the form of transcendence, as of wholes relative to their parts, and such transcendence can no doubt be found in some form almost universally.

As regards social roles the focus so far has been on the king (F4+), representative of society as a whole, versus the priest (F1), a part of society, but of course non-centralised societies lack anything like a king. But even if society as a whole is not represented by an individual occupying a permanent role, this does not mean that society as a whole does not exist, either for the analyst or the people under study. The most obvious way for a society as a whole to manifest itself is simply to assemble. A potential divide always exists between social and religious phenomena pertaining to such assemblies and those occurring in other contexts. Thus Mauss, like Durkheim in the *Elementary Forms*, drew a sharp distinction between two sorts of totemic cult. 'Normally totemism is not a cult of the tribe as a whole', but rather of its segments, its moieties, phratries or clans (*M*: 216). On the other hand, for initiation rituals, at fixed periods of the year, 'the tribe gathers as a whole', each clan contributing its specialised service, usually in public, the whole multi-day event constituting 'totemic theatre' (*M*: 221). So the rituals pertaining to the whole are distinct from those relating to the segment, the number and nature of the segments being irrelevant.

The totality in question will not usually be solely a matter of social morphology or demography. Let us consider again the categories of time and space. As Hubert's subtitle indicated, his essay was concerned not with time in general but with its representation in religion and magic – indeed in his review of it, Mauss criticises Hubert for not

142					*Categories and Classifications*

clarifying the relation between religious time and secular duration (07, I: 51). Hubert's autobiographical note (1979: 206) confirms that he intended the essay as a first step towards a work on festivals, and in practice its focus is largely on annual ritual calendars. Critical dates, especially festivals, cut up the annual cycle into blocks of time each with its own distinct character, and as Mauss puts it in his summary (07, I: 51), 'a festival is symbolic of the whole duration which it commands, inaugurates or ends'. It follows that a New Year festival symbolises the year as a whole. Hubert does not discuss this point, which is perhaps obvious, but we see again a potential divide, this time between temporal whole and part, between year and seasons (or periods defined less naturalistically than seasons). One recalls how Arjuna's journey seems to encompass the three lower-valued journeys.

A festival that assembles all the members of a tribe concentrates what is normally dispersed over a larger territory. The assembly place need not, of course, be in the geometrical centre of the territory, though such a solution will, pragmatically, minimise travel for all concerned, as well as being schematically neatest. Similarly, the larger territory need not be conceptualised as segmented into four regions associated with cardinal points, though such conceptions are common enough. Mauss was particularly interested in the category of space, on which he reflected from his earliest writings. Reviewing a book on Buddhist prayer wheels and circular motion (98, I: 314), he comments that 'the division of the world into regions following the cardinal points is probably a fundamental idea among religious notions', that 'social consciousness attributed such and such a religious nature to such and such a part of the universe'. These points are elaborated in the light of ethnography in 1903, where different clans are linked with different sectors or directions of the tribal village or circular camp; cardinal points are sometimes involved, sometimes not, and a centre, an omphalos or navel of the earth (II: 87), may be explicit or merely implicit. We have often referred above to Mauss's 1933 response to Granet, in which he situates Hertz's interest in left and right within a wider framework (II: 145). Individual and collectivity count 'not in one but in three dimensions, or rather they count six divisions, six poles (often oriented cosmographically) or rather they even count seven, for one needs to include the centre (*ego*, self) as a point in space of a special quality, a point from which there depart the symmetrical relations (up and down, front and back, and finally right and left)'. Mauss does not quite say that the centre transcends the rest of space, but he implies it by referring to its special quality and envisaging it as the starting point for relations.

Static concepts of cardinal points were however, only one side of his interest in space: he was even more interested in the dynamic aspect, in spatial rhythms of concentration and dispersal. This was most clearly expressed in his analysis of the social morphology of the Eskimos (1906), but the idea often seems implicit. One can think of a centre as concentrated social space, a New Year as concentrated social time, a quintessence as concentrated substance. Mauss ends his review of Hubert's essay on time by suggesting that in their practical aspects, religious calendars 'derive from a great law which guarantees not only religious life but social life in its entirety: the law of collective rhythm of activity, of activity that has a rhythm in order to be social'. In the context of his essay Hubert naturally could not develop this 'excessively productive idea'.[26]

The most fundamental aspect of this productivity is closely related to the social morphology. When society concentrates so as to manifest itself as a whole, it also generates the idea of the sacred, and when it disperses into its parts it reverts to the profane (Chapter 4 above). This is how Hubert and Mauss can talk of 'the identity of the sacred and the social' (08, I: 17). The sacred is, as it were, the concentrated social.

Mauss's best-known reflections on totality are summed up in the much discussed phrase 'total social fact' (Karsenti 1994; Gofman 1998). As we saw in Chapter 1, he was thinking of gatherings that bring together the whole of society, past, present and future, and everything associated with it. On such occasions everything mixes in, 'all sorts of institutions: religious; juridical and moral – the latter being political and familial at the same time; economic – which presuppose particular forms of production and consumption, or rather of prestations and distribution; without counting the aesthetic phenomena to which these facts lead,[27] and the morphological phenomena that are manifested by these institutions' (25 *SA*: 147). The list of types of social fact essentially follows the would-be exhaustive classification used by the *Année* (Chapter 6 above), omitting only the awkward category Miscellaneous. Total social facts are not covered as such in the *Manuel*, which follows the *Année sociologique* classification in reverse order from social morphology up as far as religion, but we know from Mauss's 1934 sketch of 'General Sociology' (III: 303ff.) that he situated them under that rubric (subheading 'Tradition'). Indeed he thought that instead of total phenomena they might be called general ones, though this label was less satisfactory (25, *SA*: 274; 34, II: 118). One can suppose that, when he thought of total social facts, it was the north-west American potlatch that first came to mind, much as when he thought of strict-sense religion it was no doubt sacrifice.

Chapter 6 argued that General Sociology can be seen as the F4+ rubric in the *AS* classification, but we now perhaps see more fully how the rubric relates to the notion of totality. As Mauss himself saw, one advantage of studying total social facts was that they were likely to be more universal than the various local institutions or institutional themes that composed them (25 *SA*: 276). In other words, festivals of the total type are more universal than Indo-European kings.

Although Mauss was fascinated by total social facts, since their religious aspect was only one of their aspects among others, it makes sense that he did not refer to them even under broad-sense religion. He agreed that, if one really wants to, one can in many societies talk of all traditions by starting from religion and morality, but such a view takes the colouring for the thing itself. Religion and morality are only the covering and not the foundation of the traditions that, together with education proper, ensure the handing on of social cohesion (34, III: 330).

The Indo-European separation of F4+ from the rest of the ideology is merely one form of a wider distinction between ideas and behaviour relating to totalities and those from more specialised domains of culture. But the same argument can be approached from another direction. Totalities are often articulated into sharply distinct elements, and to start from the elements rather than the whole is to think about classification. The categories 'totality' and 'class' are almost correlative. In a primitive classification the groups into which things in general are sorted form 'a single totality (*un seul et même tout*)'; classifications exist to 'unify knowledge', and the unity of knowledge is 'nothing other than the very unity of the collectivity extended to the universe' (03, II: 82, 84). As Durkheim put it (*EF*: 630), primitive classifications rest on the profound principle that 'the concept of totality is only the abstract form of the concept of society'.

In the course of human history, Durkheim and Mauss argue, these classifications tend to lose their isomorphism with social structure, but whether or not this happens, the remainder of the system tends to be used for divination. To reverse the perspective, at the basis of every system of divination there is, at least implicitly, a system of classification (03, II: 79). It is as if the diviner peeps into the operations of the cosmos, as they bear on a particular case. The more one thinks about the relations between primitive classifications and divination, the less surprising is Mauss's choice of label.

Thus the Indo-Europeans are not a bad test case with which to think about the problems of defining religion. Although it was the association between Duryodhana and magic that provided the starting point, my main focus has not been on the contrast between religion and magic (with the associated oppositions such as public and private, personal and impersonal, spiritual and material)[28]. It has been rather on the need to distinguish two aspects of religion. The lower-ranking aspect, the more terrestrial, focuses on the priest, and is probably closer to our prototype concept of religion (one can think of Vedic sac-rifice).[29] The other aspect, more cosmological and encompassing, focuses on the sacred king, if he exists, or on comparable symbols or contexts of totality. For someone who aims to define religion, part of the problem is that total social facts by definition fuse religious social facts with those from other rubrics. So it is too simple to say, in the lan-guage of the functions, that religion relates to F1 plus one fifth of F4+.[30] It is not merely that the latter fraction is in principle fused with the other fractions within F4+, but that as the highest ranking rubric apart from the transcendent one, it tends to contribute its religious colouring to the rest. This is why traditional ideologies tend to be thought of as religious in a general sense. For instance, when analysing the caste system Dumont takes for granted that 'in most societies it is religion that supplies the view of the whole' (1979: 92).

Concluding remarks

Whatever importance may, for other reasons, attach to the definition of religion and of the sacred, one can hardly hope to understand Durkheimian sociology without wrestling with them (cf. Prades 1987), and there is of course a large relevant literature by compara-tive religionists (e.g., Paden 1998). Rather than directly engaging with this problem, I hope to have shown that, in spite of all the pressures to think of religion as a single concept, it actually brings together two ele-ments that are theoretically distinct and that in some cultural con-texts have been conceived as distinct. Arjuna, Romulus and Śibi really do contrast with Yudhiṣṭhira, Numa and Aṣṭaka.

Such a division within the concept of religion has implications for debates about the categories of the sacred and of *mana*. Terrestrial reli-gion would pertain primarily to humanity's dealings with the sacred, while cosmology or cosmological religion would pertain rather to the sacred in itself. From this point of view it is not surprising that the two should be so interrelated that the distinction between them has not been obvious in the past – so that, to mention just one consequence, trifunctionalists have wanted to see them as the Mitra and Varuṇa aspects of a single domain within the Indo-European ideology.

The language of the Indo-European functions has been so useful above that I end with an idea formulated in the same language, which is offered as preliminary and suggestive rather than well worked out. The fourth function was postulated for various reasons relating to Indo-European comparativism. It was conceived as relating to the other world, to otherness relative to our ordinary everyday world, and it soon became clear that it had positive and negative aspects. All of this analysis was quite independent of any bearing on general questions about magic and religion. However, if this chapter is right, religion in its transcendent, encompassing, totalising, socially approved aspect relates to the positive aspect of the fourth function, while magic with its tendency towards materialism, atomism, privacy and the disreputable relates to the negative aspect of the function. Perhaps the otherness shared by the two aspects is more fundamental than the question of whether theoretical primacy is given to the sacredness of the former or the *mana* of the latter, to Durkheim's approach or to Mauss's.

Notes

1. Hubert is referring to his own work of 1905, and to the remarks in PC (summarised II: 86–7) on spatial conceptions among the Zuñi and other peoples.

2. Cited by Lévi-Strauss (1962: 18); cf. *SA*: 69.

3. On the whole, the religion-magic distinction fits reasonably well with the distinction that I found among the Thulung Rai in East Nepal between priest and medium (Allen 1976).

4. The poetic phrasing reminds me of Mauss's 1924 remark on 'moons, dead, pale and obscure'. Etymologically the word 'profane' means 'in front of (i.e., outside) the temple (*fanum*)', as the writers evidently knew.

5. Another formulation: '*mana* is at once the notion of a power, a cause, a force, a substance, a milieu' (08, I: 19). The discussion of Hubert (1904: xlv ff.) is worth noting: 'taboo, that is to say interdiction, is more specially religious than *mana*, that is to say force'.

6. Mauss would have felt the etymology: Latin *nebula* means 'cloud'.

7. The choice must have been influenced by other factors too, notably the teaching of Mauss's Indology teacher Sylvain Lévi (35, III: 538; cf. Strenski 1997).

8. Draupadī is not in fact a sister of the Pāṇḍava brothers but of their general.

9. I hope eventually to cover this material in greater detail and more philologically in the context of a comparison between Greece and India, so I here (after some hesitation) give references in the form most convenient to most readers. Rather than citing the Sanskrit chapter and verse numbers, I refer to pages in the translation (1973–78) of the first third of the Critical Edition of the *Mahābhārata* by van Buitenen (abbreviated as vB).

10. According to vB, I: 153–4, Prince Duryodhana, evil-spirited, evil-minded disgracer of the Kurus, was 'born on earth from a portion of Kali [demon of the last and worst cosmic era]; he was a creature of discord, hated by all the world'.

11. Hubert and Mauss emphasise that their sources represent only one tradition of early Indian magic. Were they aware of the Tantric tradition?

12. The passage plays on the Latin verb *facio* 'make, do', which lies behind the French *faire, font, efficace*, as well as Latin *factum*.

13. The goddess Nirṛti is another personified abstraction, comparable to Kṛtyā. However, both of them, indeed like the demons who summon Duryodhana, show the relatively weak personification that Hubert and Mauss see as characterising demonic persons (*SA*: 98–99).

14. Though it is often rendered 'ford', Sanskrit *tīrtha* means a place where it is religiously meritorious to bathe, not necessarily a place at which to cross a river. The 'crossing' in question is metaphysical.

15. The journeys are listed in the order the reader encounters them.
16. A full study of the six journeys would have to look at the cognate material in Greek epic, which is deliberately ignored here. Cf. Allen 1998c and 2000.
17. Both of these temporal patterns need to be related to that of the four eras of Hindu cosmic time. Their duration and rank steadily decline, but they are transcended by the Creator Brahmā.
18. It can probably be argued that Arjuna's journey, which takes him outside this world, contrasts with Yudhishṭhira's as *mokṣa* contrasts with *dharma*; but these are complex Hindu concepts, and the argument lies beyond my present scope.
19. This section contains the statement, which I do not understand, that 'everything that is religious is *mana*; everything that is *mana* is religious *and* sacred.'
20. Table I of that paper should have been printed with Romulus in row 2 indented.
21. In fact Romulus is often said to have acted by means of *auguria*, but the two words are semantically close.
22. In earlier incarnations, this book, called *Mitra-Varuna*, was dedicated to 'my teachers Marcel Mauss and Marcel Granet'.
23. In a phrase that has quite often been cited, Hubert (1904: xlvii) defined religion as 'the administration of the sacred'. The phrase applies excellently to the priest, less so to the king. The king embodies the sacred, rather than administering it.
24. Since Duryodhana (F4–) is linked with magic, one might look for the same link in the case of the devalued outsider Roman kings. The central member of the triad, Servius, whose name implies his origins as a slave (*servus*), is particularly associated with the goddess Diana, who is herself not Roman (Dumézil 1974: 409–13). Linked with slaves in general, she is served by the slave-priest of Nemi, the *rex nemorensis*, made famous by Frazer's *Golden Bough*. Hubert and Mauss mention the cult of Diana in the magic of the Middle Ages (*SA*: 16).
25. One cannot help recalling Lucifer, whose place in European magic is mentioned by Hubert and Mauss (04, *SA*: 77).
26. In India, the rhythm of concentration and dispersal is prominent in the interrelated soteriologies of yoga and Sāṃkhya (cf. Allen 1998e), where the practitioner tries to reverse the cosmogonic processes of diversification.
27. 'Aesthetics remains still very material, even when it appears very ideal [i.e., a matter of ideas]; plastic aesthetics is scarcely differentiated from technology' (*M*: 15).
28. Cf. Lévi-Strauss (1962: 292–93): 'in a sense one can say that religion consists in a *humanisation of natural laws*, and magic consists in a *naturalisation of human actions*'.
29. I mean Vedic sacrifices made to gods and conducted by brahmans. I am not sure whether Hubert and Mauss were right to connect so closely this sort of sacrifice with sacrifices of the god, for instance the mythic cosmogonic self-sacrifice of Puruṣa.
30. If F4+ really represents the totality, it may contain within it the whole fivefold structure – including therefore a sort of 'F4+ squared', within which F1 will contribute a further one twenty-fifth to the whole. Logically the sequence continues indefinitely.

Appendix 1

MAUSS'S LECTURING

In the following list, apart from the Indology at the start of Mauss's career, the titles have been adapted or abstracted from the course summaries given in the *Oeuvres*. They are only approximate, and from the fact that two courses are listed under the same title it does not follow that they addressed exactly the same questions or used identical material. The titles are followed by the last two digits of the year in which the course finished, so that 03 refers to the academic year 1902/03. Mauss usually gave two courses per year at the Ecole Pratique des Hautes Etudes (section des sciences religieuses), but not always. He gave none in 1921/22, when he was ill, or in 1925/26. From 1931 onwards he also gave one or two lectures per week at the Collège de France. His annual lecture course at the Institut d'Ethnologie (1926–39) is ignored here.

Indology: Outline of Indian religious history, Hindu philosophies and Vedantic texts, and history of yoga 01 (see Fournier 1994: 181).
Prayer and oral ritual among native Australians 02, 03; 10, 11, 12, 13, 14; 21, 23, 24, 25, 27, 28, 29, 30, 31, 32.
Magic in Melanesia 03; magic and religion in Melanesia 38.
Magic in its relation to religion 04 (interrupted by instructions for ethnography of technology and folklore in Korea); magic alone 05.
Kinship and totemism among Eskimos 04, 05.
Kinship and religion among NW Amerindians (and in Australia) 06. Secret societies among Kwakiutl (NW Amerindians) 06. Potlatch in same area 11, 12.
Taboo, esp. Polynesian 07; esp. Maori 10.
General instructions on ethnography 08.
Religion in Africa 07, 08, 09; ethnographic questionnaire for French Central and West Africa 07, 08; Ashanti kinship and religion 25; ethnography of French West Africa 27; Ashanti, esp. their art, 32.
Kinship and religion among Pueblo native Americans 08.

Potlatch and exchange in New Guinea 13, and among Bantu 14; potlatch in Melanesia 21, and secret societies there 23; Trobriand exchange 34.

Ethnography of Marind Anim and/or Kiwai of New Guinea 28, 29, 30, 31.

'General phenomena' in tribal social life 31.

Durkheim on civic and professional morality 32.

The notion of the primitive 32.

North and Northeast Asia (esp. Gilyak) 33; palaeoasiatic cosmology 34, esp. Ainu 35, 36; esp. shamanism 37.

Maori religion (based on work of Hertz) 33, 34, 35, 36, 37. Polynesian religion and cosmology, esp. Maori and Hawaiian 34, 36, 38 (esp. games), 39; esp. Maori 35, esp. Hawaiian 37, 38.

Germanic civilisation (based on work of Hubert) 35, 36, 37, 38, 39, 40.

Games and cosmology in native North America 39; esp. Zuñi 40.

BIBLIOGRAPHY

(An asterisk indicates the original publication of a paper included in this volume.)

Allen, N.J. 1972, 'The vertical dimension in Thulung classification', *JASO* 3: 81–94.

———. 1976, 'Approaches to illness in the Nepalese hills', in *Social anthropology and medicine*, ed. J.B. Loudon, London, 500–52.

———. 1982, 'A dance of relatives', *JASO* 13: 139–46.

*———. 1985, 'The category of the person: a reading of Mauss's last essay', in *The category of the person in anthropology*, eds M. Carrithers et al., Cambridge. (Chapter 1)

———. 1986, 'Tetradic theory: an approach to kinship', *JASO* 17: 87–109.

———. 1987, 'The ideology of the Indo-Europeans: Dumézil's theory and the idea of a fourth function', *International journal of moral and social studies* 2: 23–39.

———. 1989a, 'The evolution of kinship terminologies', *Lingua* 77: 173–185.

———. 1989b, 'Assimilation of alternate generations', *JASO* 20: 45–55.

———. 1991, 'Some gods of pre-Islamic Nuristan', *Revue de l'histoire des religions* 208: 141–68.

*———. 1994, '*Primitive classification*: the argument and its validity', in *Debating Durkheim*, eds W. Pickering and H. Martins, London, 40–65. (Chapter 2)

*———. 1995, '*The division of labour* and the notion of primitive society: a Maussian perspective', *Social anthropology* 3: 49–59. (Chapter 3)

———. 1996a, 'The hero's five relationships: a proto-Indo-European story', in *Myth and myth-making*, ed. J. Leslie, London, 1–20.

———. 1996b, 'Romulus and the fourth function' in *Indo-European religion after Dumézil*, ed. E.C. Polomé, Washington, 13–36.

*———. 1998a, 'Effervescence and the origins of human society', in *Essays on Durkheim's Elementary Forms*, eds N.J. Allen, W.S.F. Pickering and W. Watts Miller, London, 149–61. (Chapter 4)

———. 1998b, 'The prehistory of Dravidian-type terminologies', in

Transformations of kinship, eds M. Godelier, T. Trautmann and F. Tjon Sie Fat, Washington, 314–31.

———. 1998c, 'The Indo-European prehistory of yoga', *International journal of Hindu studies* 2: 1–20.

*———. 1998d, 'Mauss and the categories', *Durkheimian Studies* 4: 39–50. (Chapter 5)

———. 1998e, 'The category of substance: a Maussian theme revisited', in *Marcel Mauss: a centenary tribute*, eds W. James and N.J. Allen, Oxford, 175–91.

———. 1998f, 'Varnas, colours, and functions: expanding Dumézil's schema', *Zeitschrift für Religionswissenschaft* 6: 163–77.

———. 1999a, 'Arjuna and the second function: a Dumézilian crux', *Journal of the Royal Asiatic Society, series 3*, 9: 403–18.

———. 1999b, 'Hinduism, structuralism and Dumézil', in *Miscellanea Indo-Europea*, ed. E.C. Polomé, Washington, 241–60.

———. 2000, 'Argos and Hanuman: Odysseus' dog in the light of the *Mahābhārata*', *Journal of Indo-European studies* 28: 3–16.

*———. in press, 'Reflections on Mauss and classification', *Body and society*. (Chapter 6)

Anon. 1867, 'Catégorie', in *Grand dictionnaire universel du XIXe siècle*, ed. Pierre Larousse, vol. 3, Paris, 575–77.

———. 1940, 'In memoriam: Stefan Sigmunt Czarnowski (1879–1937)', *Annales sociologiques* Sér. B 1, 4: 1–5.

Ardener, E. 1989, *The voice of prophecy and other essays*, ed. M. Chapman, Oxford.

Aston, M.P. 1978, 'The French school of sociology 1890–1920', D.Phil. thesis, University of Oxford.

Atran, S. 1990, *Cognitive foundations of natural history: towards an anthropology of science*, Cambridge.

Baldick, J. 1994, *Homer and the Indo-Europeans*, London.

Barnard, A. 1994, 'Rules and prohibitions: the form and content of human kinship', in *Companion encyclopaedia of anthropology: humanity, culture and social life*, ed. T. Ingold, London.

Barnes, J.A. 1966, 'Durkheim's Division of Labour in Society', *Man* 1: 158–75.

Benveniste, E. 1966, *Problèmes de linguistique générale*, Paris.

Berthoud, G. and Busino, B. eds, 1996, *Mauss: hier et aujourd'hui* [= *Revue européenne des sciences sociales* 34], Geneva.

Besnard, P. ed., 1979, 'Les Durkheimiens', *Revue française de sociologie* 20, 1.

———. ed., 1983, *The sociological domain: the Durkheimians and the founding of French sociology*, Cambridge.

———. Borlandi, M. and Vogt, P. eds, 1993, *Division du travail et lien social: Durkheim un siècle après*, Paris.

Bloor, D. 1982, 'Durkheim and Mauss revisited: classification and the sociology of knowledge', *Studies in the history and philosophy of science* 13: 267–97.

Borlandi, M. 1993, 'Durkheim lecteur de Spencer', *Division du travail et lien social*, ed. P. Besnard et al., Paris, 67–109.

Brown, C.H. 1984, *Language and living things: uniformities in folk classification and naming*, New Brunswick.

Caillé, A. 1996, 'Ni holisme ni individualisme méthodologiques: Marcel Mauss et le paradigme du don', in *Mauss: hier et aujourd'hui*, eds G. Berthoud and B. Busino, Geneva, 181–224.

Carrithers, M., Collins, S. and Lukes, S. eds, 1985, *The category of the person in anthropology, philosophy, history*, Cambridge.

Cazeneuve, J. 1958, 'Les Zuñis dans l'oeuvre de Durkheim et de Mauss', *Revue philosophique* 83: 452–61.

––––––. 1968a, *Sociologie de Marcel Mauss*, Paris.

––––––. 1968b, *Mauss*, Paris.

Chapman, M., McDonald, M. and Tonkin, E. 1989, 'Introduction' in *History and ethnicity*, eds E. Tonkin, M. McDonald and M. Chapman, London.

Clark, T.N. 1973, *Prophets and patrons: the French university and the emergence of the social sciences*, Cambridge MA.

Collins, S. 1985, 'Categories, concepts or predicaments? Remarks on Mauss's use of philosophical terminology', *The category of the person in anthropology*, eds M. Carrithers et al., Cambridge, 46–82.

Condominas, G. 1972, 'Marcel Mauss, père de l'ethnographie française', *Critique* 297: 118–39; 301: 487–504.

Cushing, F. 1896, 'Outlines of Zuñi creation myths', *Annual report of the Bureau of Ethnology*, Washington.

di Donato, R. 1983, 'Di Apollon Sonore e di alcuni suoi antenati: Georges Dumézil e l'epica greca arcaica', *Opus* 2: 401–12.

Diaz-Estevez, J. 1979, 'The work of Marcel Mauss: an interpretation', D. Phil. thesis, University of Oxford.

Doroszewski, W. 1933, 'Quelques remarques sur les rapports de la sociologie et de la linguistique: Durkheim et F. de Saussure', *Journal de Psychologie* 30: 82–91.

Dubuisson, D. 1991, 'Contribution à une épistémologie dumézilienne: l'idéologie', *Revue de l'histoire des religions* 208: 123–40.

Duby, G. 1978, *Les trois ordres ou l'imaginaire du féodalisme*, Paris.

Dumézil, G. 1941, *Jupiter, Mars, Quirinus*, Paris.

––––––. 1958, *L'idéologie tripartie des Indo-Européens*, Brussels.

––––––. 1968, *Mythe et épopée vol. 1*, Paris.

––––––. 1971, *Mythe et épopée vol. II*, Paris.

––––––. 1972, *Mythe et épopée vol. III*, Paris.

––––––. 1974, *La religion romaine archaïque*, 2nd edn, Paris.

––––––. 1975, *Fêtes romaines d'été et d'automne*, Paris.

––––––. 1977, *Les dieux souverains des Indo-européens*, Paris.

––––––. 1981, *Georges Dumézil (Cahiers pour un temps)*, Paris.

––––––. 1982, *Apollon sonore et autres essais*, Paris.

––––––. 1987, *Georges Dumézil: entretiens avec Didier Eribon*, Paris.

Dumont, L. 1972, 'Une science en devenir', *L'Arc* 48, (written in 1952): 8–21 [reprinted in idem 1983, *Essais sur l'individualisme*, Paris, 167–86].

––––––. 1979, *Homo hierarchicus*, édn Tel, Paris.

––––––. 1983, *Essais sur l'individualisme: une perspective anthropologique sur l'idéologie moderne*, Paris.

Durkheim, E. 1991, *De la division du travail social*, Paris (orig. 1893).

———. 1895, *Les règles de la méthode sociologique*, Paris.

———. 1898, 'La prohibition de l'inceste et ses origines', *Année sociologique* 1: 1–70.

———. 1968, *Les formes élémentaires de la vie religieuse: le système totémique en Australie*, 5th edn, Paris (orig. 1912).

———. 1994, *Durkheim on religion*, ed. W. Pickering, Atlanta.

———. 1998, *Lettres à Marcel Mauss*, eds P. Besnard and M. Fournier, Paris.

——— and Mauss, M. 1903, 'De quelques formes primitives de classification', *Année sociologique* 6: 1–72 (for translation see R. Needham 1963).

Engler, R. 1967, *Cours de linguistique générale de F. de Saussure*, éd. critique, Wiesbaden.

Favre, P. 1983, 'The absence of political sociology in the Durkheimian classifications of the social sciences', in *The sociological domain*, ed. P. Besnard, Cambridge, 199–216.

Fortes, M. 1973, 'On the concept of the person among the Tallensi', in *La notion de personne en Afrique noire*, Paris, 283–319.

———. 1983, *Rules and the emergence of society* (Royal Anthropological Institute Occasional Paper 39), London.

Fournier, M. 1994, *Marcel Mauss*, Paris.

Fox, J. 1979 – see Mauss 1906.

Fox, R. 1980, *The red lamp of incest*, London.

Frede, M. 1987, *Essays in ancient philosophy*, Oxford.

Freedman, M. 1975, 'Marcel Granet, 1884–1940: sociologist', introductory essay in M. Granet (orig. 1922), *The religion of the Chinese people*, tr. and ed. M. Freedman, Oxford.

Godelier, M. 1996, *L'énigme du don*, Paris.

Gofman, A. 1998. 'A vague but suggestive concept: the "total social fact"', in *Marcel Mauss: a centenary tribute*, eds W. James and N.J. Allen, Oxford, 63–70.

Goldschmidt, W. 1993, 'On the relationship between biology and anthropology', *Man* 28: 341–59.

Granet, M. 1968, *La pensée chinoise*, Paris (orig. 1934).

———. 1973, 'Right and left in China', in *Right and left: essays in dual symbolic classification*, ed. R. Needham, Chicago, (orig. 1933).

———. 1939, 'Catégories matrimoniales et relations de proximité dans la Chine ancienne', *Annales sociologiques*: 1–254.

Guthrie, W. 1975, *History of Greek Philosophy*, vol. *IV*, Cambridge.

Hamelin, O. 1927, *Le système de Renouvier*, Paris.

Hamilton, P. 1990, *Emile Durkheim: critical assessments*, 4 vols, London.

Héran, F. 1996, 'Figures et légendes de la parenté', Doctorat d'état, Université de Paris V.

———. 1998, 'De Granet à Lévi-Strauss', *Social anthropology* 6: 1–60, 169–201, 309–30.

Hocart, A.M. 1970, 'Kinship systems', in *The life-giving myth*, ed. R. Needham, London (orig. 1937).

Hubert, H. 1904, 'Introduction à la traduction française' in *Manuel d'histoire des religions*, ed. P.-D. Chantepie de la Saussaye, 2ⁿᵈ edn, Paris.

———. 1979, 'Texte autobiographique de Henri Hubert', in *Revue française de sociologie* 20: 205–7.

———, *Essay on time: a brief study of the representation of time in religion and magic*, ed. R. Parkin, tr. R. Parkin and J. Redding, Oxford, 1999 (French orig. 1905).

Isambert, F.-A. 1976, 'L'élaboration de la notion de sacré dans l'"école" Durkheimienne', *Archives de sciences sociales des religions* 21, 42: 35–56.

———. 1982, *Le sens du sacré: fête et religion populaire*, Paris.

———. 1983, 'At the frontier of folklore and sociology: Hubert, Hertz and Czarnowski, founders of a sociology of folk religion', in *The sociological domain*, ed. P. Besnard, Cambridge.

Jakobson, R. 1971, 'Retrospect', in *Selected Writings, vol.2: word and language*, The Hague.

James, W. and Allen N.J. eds, 1998, *Marcel Mauss: a centenary tribute*, Oxford.

Karady, V. 1968, 'Présentation de l'édition', in M. Mauss, *Œuvres*, vol. I, i–liii.

———. 1982, 'Le problème de la légitimité dans l'organisation de l'ethnologie française', *Revue française de sociologie* 23: 17–35.

Karsenti, B. 1994, *Marcel Mauss: le fait social total*, Paris.

———. 1997, *L'homme total: sociologie, anthropologie et philosophie chez Marcel Mauss*, Paris.

———. 1998, 'The Maussian shift: a second foundation for sociology in France', in *Marcel Mauss: a centenary tribute*, eds W. James and N.J. Allen, Oxford, 71–82.

Kensinger, K.M. 1985, 'An emic model of Cashinahua marriage', in *Marriage practices in lowland South America*, ed. K.M. Kensinger, Chicago.

Knight, C. 1991, *Blood relations: menstruation and the origins of culture*, New Haven and London.

Knight, C., Power C. and Watts, I. 1995, 'The human symbolic revolution: a Darwinian account', *Cambridge archaeological journal* 5: 75–114.

Kuper, A. 1988, *The invention of primitive society: transformations of an illusion*, London.

Lacey, A. 1995, 'Categories' in *Oxford companion to philosophy*, ed. T. Honderich, Oxford, 125–6.

La Fontaine, J.S. 1985, *Initiation: ritual drama and secret knowledge across the world*, Manchester.

La notion de personne en Afrique noire, Paris, 1973.

Leach, E. 1954, *Political systems of highland Burma*, London.

Leacock, S. 1954, 'The ethnological theory of Marcel Mauss', *American Anthropologist* 56: 58–73.

Lee, H.D.P. 1955, *Plato: the Republic*, Harmondsworth.

Lévi-Strauss, C. 1947, 'La sociologie française', in *La sociologie au XXe siècle*, vol. 2, eds G. Gurvitch and W.E. Moore, Paris.

———. 1950, *Introduction à l'œuvre de Marcel Mauss*, in M. Mauss, *Sociologie et anthropologie*, Paris.

———. 1962, *La pensée sauvage*, Paris.

Lienhardt, R.G. 1964, *Social Anthropology*, London.

Lourandos, H. 1988, 'Palaeopolitics: resource intensification in Aboriginal Australia and Papua New Guinea', in *Hunters and gatherers: history, evolution and social change*, eds T. Ingold, D. Riches and J. Woodburn, Oxford.

Lukes, S. 1973, *Emile Durkheim, his life and his work: a historical and critical study*, Harmondsworth.

———. 1996, 'Quelques réflexions sur le *Mauss* de Fournier', in *Mauss: hier et aujourd'hui*, eds G. Berthoud and B. Busino, Geneva, 39–44.

Lyon, M. L. 1997, 'The material body, social processes and emotion: *Techniques of the Body* revisited', *Body and society* 3: 83–101.

Malinowski, B. 1927, *Sex and repression in savage society*, London.

Martelli, S. 1996, 'Mana ou sacré? La contribution de Marcel Mauss à la fondation de la sociologie religieuse', in *Mauss: hier et aujourd'hui*, eds G. Berthoud and B. Busino, Geneva, 51–66.

Mauss, M. 1906, 'Essai sur les variations saisonnières des Eskimo: étude de morphologie sociale', *Année sociologique* 9: 39–132 [tr. by J.J. Fox as *Seasonal variations of the Eskimo*, London, 1979].

———. 1924, 'Appréciation sociologique du bolchevisme', in *Revue de métaphysique et de morale* 31: 103–32 [reprinted in *Ecrits politiques*, Paris, 1997].

———. 1928, 'Alice Robert Hertz', in R. Hertz, *Sociologie religieuse et folklore*, Paris, xix-xx.

———. 1964, 'Discussion', tr. by D. Hymes as 'On Language and primitive forms of classification', in *Language in culture and society*, ed. D. Hymes, New York, 125–27 (orig. 1923).

———. 1968–69, *Œuvres*, vols. I-III (prés. V. Karady), Paris.

———. 1973, *Sociologie et anthropologie*, 5th edn, Paris (1st edn 1950).

———. 1989, *Manuel d'ethnographie*, 3rd edn, Paris (1st edn 1947).

———. 1996, 'L'œuvre de Mauss par lui-même', in *Mauss: hier et aujourd'hui*, eds G. Berthoud and B. Busino, Geneva, 225–36 [translations in P. Besnard ed. 1983, and as 'An intellectual self-portrait' in *Marcel Mauss*, eds W. James and N.J. Allen, 1998, 29–42].

McNeill, W.H. 1995, *Keeping together in time: dance and drill in human history*, Cambridge MA.

Mellars, P. and Stringer C. eds, 1989, *The human revolution: behavioural and biological perspectives on the origins of modern humans*, Edinburgh.

Mithen, S. 1996, *The prehistory of mind: a search for the origins of art, religion and science*, London.

Morgan, L.H. 1871, *Systems of consanguinity and affinity of the human family*, Washington D.C.

Murray, S.O. ed., 1989, 'A 1934 interview with Marcel Mauss', *American ethnologist* 16: 163–8.

Needham, R. 1963, 'Introduction', in E. Durkheim and M. Mauss, *Primitive classification*, (tr. and ed. R. Needham), London.

———. 1974, *Remarks and inventions: skeptical essays about kinship*, London.

———. 1979, *Symbolic classification*, Santa Monica.

Paden, W. 1998, 'Religion, world, plurality', in *What is religion? Origins, definitions, and explanations*, eds T.A. Idinopulos and B.C. Wilson, Leiden, 91–105.

Palmer, E. 1884, 'Notes on some Australian tribes', *Journal of the Anthropological Institute* 13: 276–334.

Palmer, N.F. 1998, 'Cosmic quaternities in the *Roman de Fauvel*', in *Fauvel Studies*, eds M. Bent and A. Wathey, Oxford.

Paulme, D. 1989, 'Préface à la troisième édition (1989)', in M. Mauss *Manuel d'ethnographie*, Paris.

Pickering, W.S.F. 1984, *Durkheim's sociology of religion: themes and theories*, London.

———. 1998, 'Mauss's Jewish background: a biographical essay', *Marcel Mauss: a centenary tribute*, eds W. James and N.J. Allen, Oxford, 42–60.

Powell, J.W. 1896, 'Administrative report', *Annual report of the Bureau of Ethnology*, Washington.

Prades, J.A. 1987, *Persistance et métamorphose du sacré: actualiser Durkheim et repenser la modernité*, Paris.

Quéré, L. 1994, 'Présentation', in *L'enquête sur les catégories: de Durkheim à Sacks*, eds B. Fradin, L. Quéré and J. Widmer, Paris, 7–40.

Quiatt, D. and Reynolds, V. 1993, *Primate behaviour: information, social knowledge and the evolution of culture*, Cambridge.

Rees, A. and Rees, B. 1961, *Celtic heritage*, London.

Reynolds, V. 1967, *The apes, the gorilla, chimpanzee, orangutan and gibbon: their history and their world*, London.

———. 1974, 'Friendship among the primates', in E. Leyton, *The compact: selected dimensions of friendship*, Newfoundland, 33–41.

Rig Veda: an anthology, 1981, ed. and tr. W. Doniger O'Flaherty, Harmondsworth.

Rushdie, S. 1999, *The ground beneath her feet*, London.

Sadowska, E. 1986, 'Stefan Czarnowski, a forerunner of Celtic Studies', *Hemispheres: studies on cultures and societies* 3: 171–94.

Saussure, F. de. 1985, *Cours de linguistique générale*, ed. T. de Mauro, Paris [tr. and ann. by R. Harris as *Course in general linguistics*, London, 1983].

Schmaus, W. 1998, 'Durkheim on the causes and functions of the categories', in *Essays on Durkheim's Elementary Forms*, eds N.J. Allen, W.S.F. Pickering and W. Watts Miller, London, 176–88.

Smith, R. 1995, 'Logic', in *The Cambridge companion to Aristotle*, ed. J. Barnes, 27–65.

Steiner, P. 1994, *La sociologie de Durkheim*, Paris.

Strenski, I. 1997, *Durkheim and the Jews of France*, Chicago.

Tarot, C. 1996, 'Du fait social de Durkheim au fait social total de Mauss: un changement de paradigme?', in *Mauss: hier et aujourd'hui*, eds G. Berthoud and B. Busino, Geneva, 113–44.

Turner, V. 1969, *The ritual process*, Harmondsworth.

van Buitenen, J. (tr.), 1973–78, *The Mahābhārata*, vols 1–3. Chicago.

Waldberg, P. 1970, 'Au fil du souvenir', in *Echanges et communications*, vol. I, eds J. Pouillon and P. Maranda, The Hague, 581–86.

Wallwork, W. 1984, 'Religion and social structure in *The Division of Labor'*,
    American Anthropologist 86: 43–64 [reprinted in Hamilton 1990].
White, D. 1997, 'Mountains of wisdom: on the interface between Siddha and
    Vidyādhara cults and the siddha orders in Medieval India', in *International journal of Hindu studies* 1: 73–95.
Yates, F.A. 1979, *The occult philosophy in the Elizabethan age*, London.

INDEX

aesthetics 5, 9, 28–30, 86, 119, 130, 143, 147; see Mauss and arts
affect 31, 51, 55, 57, 118, 125; see effervescence
Africa 4, 35; west 27, 149; north 64; Ashanti 4, 27, 149; Dahomey 25; Maasai 28; Negro 26; Morocco 35; Togo 93; Bantu 28, 150
alchemy 125
alternate generations, identification of 9, 26, 70, 82; transmission between 9, 13, 34, 97; see name
America (native, north) 4, 21, 26, 64, 120, 149; northwest 28; Haida 30; Hopi 31, 39; Iroquois 65; Kwakiutl 12, 25, 29–30; Omaha 31, 49; Pueblo 149; Sioux 49; south America 5; see Zuñi
Année sociologique 3, 6, 29; rubrics 8, 15, 22, Ch. 6; as school 16, 19, 23, 36, 66, 73 80, 122; ideas still useful 88
architecture 29
Ardener, E. 59
Aristotle 1, 14, 33, 92–5, 98, 103
Asia north-east 5, 150; west 64
astronomy 122, 133, 135; planets 9; astral mythology 48

Atran, S. 57
Australia 4, 20f, 45–8, 62, 64, 73, 79, 82, 119, 149; Arunta 26, 30, 47–49? Wotjoballuk 47, 439, 55; Kariera 80; Tasmanians 20

Baldick, J. 17
Barnard, A. 81
Barnes, J.A. 61
Benveniste, E. 28, 93
Berthoud, G. and Busino, B. 6, 91
Besnard, P. 35, 62
Biardeau, M. 130
Bible 61; biblical world 82
Bloor, D. 35
body, techniques of 98, Ch.6; in myth 113–4, 125; decoration 29, 88
Borlandi, M. 73
Brahmā 147
bricolage 30, 57
Brown, C.H. 57
Buddhism 3, 121, 142

cadre 51, 59, 102, 103, 109, 115
Caillé, A. 2, 91
cardinal points 13, 17, 48–9, 59, 107, 120, 131, 142; gods of 133, 137; see space
Carrithers, M. 7, 40

Mitra 136–7, 145; *Mitra-Varuṇa*
    147
moieties 45–7, 49, 63, 68–71,
    78–81, 87, 88, 96–7
monetisation 99
monotheism 13, 50
Morgan, L.H. 31, 63–4, 73, 81, 85
Murray, S.O. 91
music 22, 29, 93, 126; see rhythm
myth 17, 25, 50, 113–4, 118

names 13, 96, 122; fixed stock of
    25–7, 31, 34; ethnonyms 25,
    72; see souls
nation 118
Needham, R. 39–41, 51–6, 60,
    82, 99
New Guinea 120, 150
number as category 13, 30, 33,
    94–5

Paden, W. 143
palaeoanthropology 2, 12, Ch. 4
Palmer, E. 59
Palmer, N.F. 9
Paulme, D. 1, 5, 14, 99
person (as category) 7–8, Ch. 1,
    93, 95, 113, 118
Piaget, J. 74
Pickering, W.S.F. 77
pilgrimage 127–132, 146
Plato 16, 28, 112, 114–5
politics 66, 111–2, 115
Polynesia 4, 149; see Maori
possession 25, 30
potlatch 4, 29, 123, 143, 149–50;
    see festival
Powell, J.W. 60
Prades, J.A. 8, 89, 145
priesthood 28, 29, 126; flamens
    42–3; Zuñi 48–9, 59; and F1
    141, 144; see religion
primatology 66–7, 85–6

'primitive' 20–2, Ch. 3, 76–7,
    104; see evolution
primitive classification, *PC* 9–11,
    22, 27, 31–3, Ch. 2, 91, 95,
    98, Ch. 6, 129, 135, 144

quality as category 94–5, 104,
    107; see primitive
    classification
quantity as category 94–5; see
    number, totality

Quéré, L. 94
Quiatt, D. and Reynolds, V. 67, 88

Radcliffe Brown, A.R. 17
reciprocity 65–6, 70; see
    exchange
Rees, A. and Rees, B. 17
reincarnation 25–6, 29–30, 96;
    see alternate generations
relation (as category) 14, 94–7;
    syntagmatic and paradig-
    matic 42–7, 54–5, 58, 105;
    joking 96; see hierarchy
religion 3, 5, 8, 16–7, 35, Ch. 7;
    origins 77, 83–5; see
    priesthood, sacred,
    totemism
Renouvier, C. 92, 94–7
retirement 26, 30
Reynolds, V. 67, 86; see Quiatt
rhythm 29, 86, 89, 143
right and left 92, 125; see Hertz
ritual 47, 74, 65, 87, 108; clan
    and tribal 83, 88; see
    totemism, festivals,
    sacrifice
Rome 42–4, 135–7; Roman law
    27, 121; slaves 26, 147;
    Vergil 27
Romulus 136–7
Rushdie, S. 16